ADDLESTONE'S VICTORY PARK

Tracing the backgrounds of the servicemen whose names are inscribed on Addlestone's civic memorial to the First World War

The origins of the park

And some others with local connections who fell and who are not inscribed

by

Jim Knight

2012

First published 2012

Published by:
Addlestone Historical Society
20 School Lane
Addlestone
KT15 1TB

Further copies available from:
Jim Knight
13 The Paddocks
New Haw
Addlestone
Surrey KT15 3LX

ISBN: 978-0-9571057-0-6

Printed by:
Print Resources
Welwyn Garden City
Hertfordshire

Front cover: The family group photograph shows Lewis Herman Proctor, with his wife Ethel and children Leonard, age 10, Dorothy, age 4, Kenneth, age 2

In memory of my father

ALGERNON CYRIL KNIGHT D.C.M. (1888-1966)
C.S.M. 1st Battalion King's Shropshire Light Infantry

Algernon enlisted on 18 September 1906. He entered France with the British Expeditionary Force on 10 September 1914 and was discharged *'no longer physically fit for War Service'* on 30 May 1919.

> I have seen a green country, useful to the race,
> Knocked silly with guns and mines, its villages
> vanished,
> Even the last rat and last kestrel banished -
> God bless us all, this was a peculiar grace.

Edmund Blunden: 'Report on Experience'

Contents

Author's introduction and notes

Addlestone's civic memorial to the First World War (there is a fine parish memorial in St Paul's church) comprises the gardens and playing fields of Victory Park and the memorial gateway at the park's entrance on Chertsey Road. In this book, I have attempted to compile some information about each of the 142 men whose names are inscribed on the gateway's stone pillars. I have drawn on material from the Commonwealth War Graves Commission's 'Debt of Honour Register', the 'Soldiers Died in the Great War 1914-1919' database, parish records, the General Register Office, census returns and local newspaper reports. Occasionally, I have used other records for supplementary information. Two of the inscribed names have eluded me, viz. *'William Allen'*, and *'Charles Hiley'*, but I remain hopeful that some clues as to the identity of these men may be uncovered in the future.

I have presented names as found in birth or baptism records and in alphabetical order; the names inscribed on the memorial are generally so arranged, but sometimes, where the same surnames occur, they are separated from namesakes who were not related.

The Surrey Herald is the newspaper I examined at most length. Throughout the war and for a while afterwards this weekly publication, established in 1895 and still in print, chronicled the deaths, injuries, gallantry awards and civilian employment of servicemen either coming from North Surrey or with connections in that area. Frequently poignant, sometimes graphic, the reports and announcements transcribed herein seem to reflect a community's unquestioning resignation in the face of the unfolding horrors of the war, and a society whose expectations were dissimilar to those which prevail in the 21st century. Underage enlistment, as in the cases of James Fuidge and Albert Gregory, was perhaps more a matter of pride than controversy. I found 99 Victory Park names mentioned in *The Surrey Herald*, but I cannot guarantee that my trawl is entire. Sometimes an individual is referred to more than once; occasionally, there is just an 'In Memoriam'. The newspaper encouraged families to send in photographs of their servicemen. A good number were published and I have included those I found. Four further photographs of servicemen were obtained elsewhere and these have been duly acknowledged.

ADDLESTONE

WAR MEMORIAL

It is requested that the NAMES of all the MEN or WOMEN who died on Active Service during the Great War, residents of the Electoral Division of Addlestone and New Haw and Woodham, be sent forthwith to the Hon. Sec.,

C. H. GREGORY,
Fieldhurst,
Addlestone.

The Victory Park names appear to have been obtained by means of an advertisement in *The Surrey Herald* of 26 September 1919 (left). A list of those who were nominated was published some two months later and, barring one or two cases, it tallies with the names that were subsequently inscribed. However, *The Surrey Herald* carried several reports of fatal casualties that are not inscribed and which might have been worthy of inclusion. This prompted me to request a search of The Commonwealth War Graves Commission's 'Debt of Honour Register' using the keyword *'Addlestone'* which brought to light a few more omitted cases. Of course, people were not obliged to send in names. One may imagine that traumatization or opting for privacy caused some families not to respond. Others may have moved away or, in some cases, there may have been a lack of interest. In Appendix 1, I have assembled details of some 41 casualties whose names are not inscribed at Victory Park but who might have qualified for inclusion. No doubt, there are some further cases in this category, yet undiscovered.

Time and space have prevented me from including *The Surrey Herald's* coverage of Addlestone's Great War gallantry awards, non-fatal casualties and prisoners of war. Perhaps these can be the subject of a further project.

Victory Park - *'not financially practicable'*

THE
VILLAGE HALL
ADDLESTONE.

. A .

GREAT WAR

MEMORIAL

MEETING

(Convened by the Addlestone Chamber of Trade)

Will be held in the above Hall, on

TUESDAY, MARCH 25, 1919

Chair to be taken at 8 p.m., by

Lt. Col. SIR JOHN HUMPHERY

supported by leading local residents.

The object of the Meeting is to promote a Scheme whereby we may perpetuate the Memory of the Addle-stone 'Boys' WHO HAVE SACRI-FICED LIFE THAT WE MIGHT LIVE.

The Members of the Chamber of Trade wish this Meeting to be thoroughly Representative, and extend to ALL a hearty invitation.

A public meeting, announced in *The Surrey Herald* of 21 March 1919 (left), elected a committee under the chair of Mr Constantine Doresa, Addlestone's County Councillor. Its purpose was *'to consider and report on the provision of a war memorial for Addlestone, such memorial to take the form if practicable of a park or recreation ground, containing a suitable monument or shrine.'* The costs of the scheme were to be met by fund-raising events and public subscription, and on completion, the grounds and monument were to be transferred to the Council. The park and memorial were officially opened and conveyed some 4¼ years later.

Doresa's committee set about the task of fund-raising with great vigour. Concert parties, band concerts, whist drives, a flag day, a doorstep collection and a private subscription ball which *'included the majority of the local gentry'*, were among the events held throughout 1919 and into the summer of 1920. Subscription lists were published with the amount given ascribed to each name.

The title 'Victory Park' emerged at the next public meeting, on 27 May 1919. It was announced that £1,000 had been raised. However, the Committee had estimated that £3,000 would be needed and doubt had begun to emerge regarding the scheme's practicability.

Doresa offered a recommendation that *'...whilst such a scheme is most desirable it is not financially practicable.'* However, the meeting rejected this counsel and passed unanimously the resolution *'That the people of Addlestone pledges its confidence in the Committee, and asks them to continue their services, and that this meeting pledges itself to do its utmost to secure the necessary funds.'*

The Committee purchased the land for the park's development a few days later. A day of Peace Celebrations, *'marred only by rain'*, was held on the acquired land on 19 July and, in September, the London firm of J. Whitehead & Co. was awarded a contract for *'the supplying and erection of the memorial gates'.* The land comprised three meadows, one of which had been paid for by Norbert Chereau, the manager of Bleriot's aircraft factories at Brooklands and Addlestone, at a cost of £700. The other meadows had cost £1,700 while the final cost of the gates was expected to be £1,077. It could be asked why the Committee had committed itself at that moment to outlays amounting to over twice the amount it had in hand. One reason, presumably, was that the public seemed to have underwritten the Committee's activities while Doresa, no doubt with that pledge in mind, had advanced £1,700 as a loan *'in order that there should be somewhere on which to place the memorial.'*

FOR OUR VICTORY PARK

A GRAND

EVENING CONCERT

will be held at the

Village Hall, ADDLESTONE,

ON TUESDAY, NOV. 18th, 1919,

Commencing at 8 p.m. by

MR. PHILIP RITTE'S CONCERT PARTY.

ARTISTES :

Miss Doris Cowan (Soprano) ; Miss Jennifer Gwyn (Humoreske) ; Miss Tina Foster (Pianist and Accompanis) ; Mr. Philip Ritte (Tenor) ; Mr. Hector Gordon (Scottish Humorist) ; Mr. Will Edwards (Comedian)

Proceeds devoted to the

VICTORY PARK FUND.

TICKETS—5/-, 4/-, Numbered and Reserved ; 3/6 and 2/- Reserved (including Tax) ; to be obtained of the Committee and Mr. Wyles, and Mr. S. Clarke, where plan of seats may be seen.

PLEASE NOTE—A Whist Drive will be held at the Village Homes on Wednesday, November 26th. Eight Prizes. Tickets 1/9

The next public meeting took place over a year later, on 8 June 1920: *'The attendance, however, was not large.'* Very little more money had come in - the amount now totalled £1,545. The memorial gates had been erected and paid for, but the balance in hand for clearing Doresa's £1,700 loan was £297. Members of the Committee explained that the memorial gates *'should be unveiled and dedicated with due ceremony'* and that event took place on 14 July 1920. However, the park's pathways had not been completed and, in any event, the Committee *'felt that if they did open it, and admitted everybody free, those who had not yet subscribed would not then do so, and they would have very little chance of raising the balance.'*

The Surrey Herald went silent on the matter. The park remained closed while weeds grew in the vicinity of the memorial and on the unpaved pathways. Eventually, in March 1923, the newspaper carried news that Doresa was to turn his loan into a gift. *'The money otherwise subscribed will be allocated to the memorial gates, the continuation of the iron fencing along the whole front of the park, and perhaps in other directions, including the possibility of a fountain for the children. Mr. Doresa's kindness will permit the accounts to be cleared, and everything satisfactorily settled, so that the Park may be handed over, free of debt, to the Urban Council, for that body to maintain it for the good of the people.'*

The official opening of Addlestone's Victory Park, and its acceptance by Chertsey Urban Council took place on Saturday 7 July 1923. The event was *'favoured with brilliant weather'* and was *'largely attended.'* A marble fountain had been erected some 30 metres inside the gates. It still stands, though currently 'dry' and the top section is missing. A plaque at the fountain's base reads *'THIS WAR MEMORIAL WAS SUBSCRIBED FOR BY THE INHABITANTS OF ADDLESTONE AND THE PARK PRESENTED TO THE PUBLIC BY C. DORESA ESQ. C.C. IN MEMORY OF HIS BELOVED WIFE WHO PASSED AWAY APRIL 21ST 1922'*

ADDLESTONE VICTORY PARK.

The official opening of the Addlestone Victory Park will take place on

Saturday, July 7th,

at 2.30 p.m.

Arrangements :

BRIEF DIVINE SERVICE.

OPENING by C. DORESA, ESQ., C C.

FORMAL ACCEPTANCE of the PARK on behalf of the Council by MR. A. FAULKNER, J.P.

Addresses by SIR PHILIP RICHARDSON, M.P , G. MALCOLM HILBERY, ESQ., and others.

C. H. GREGORY,

Hon. Secretary, Addlestone War Memorial Fund.

Doresa's wife, Florence, who had died suddenly at the age of 48 when the future of Victory Park had hung in the balance, is referred to but not named on the plaque. She was described by one of the speakers at the opening ceremony as '... *a true Christian woman, whose unselfish thoughts were ever evidenced in beneficent activities by her charm of manner and influential personality, which endeared her to the whole district.'*

The final balance sheet for the Victory Park scheme, published in April 1924, showed a total cost of £3,650. The first service of remembrance at the park took place on 11 November 1925.

Constantine Doresa (1861-1929)

was born in Cardiff, the son of a Greek immigrant who had prospered as a grain merchant in Cardiff and Bristol. Doresa settled in London and became a wealthy shipbroker, insurance agent and company director. He worked in the Government's Ministry of Shipping during the First World War. In 1913, he purchased Woodham Grange, a 120-acre estate in New Haw, near Addlestone. The estate included farmland and a large main house with a coach-house and stables. Doresa was elected County Councillor for Addlestone in 1919 and continued unopposed in that role until his death. He died at a residence he owned in the south of France and is buried in his wife's grave in the churchyard of St Nicholas, Pyrford. Woodham Grange was demolished in the mid-1930s whereupon much of the estate underwent redevelopment for housing.

In 2008, the relative value of Doresa's contribution towards the cost of Victory Park was £517,000 (share of GDP indicator).

Norbert Antoine Chereau (1863-1939) was born in France but lived in Addlestone

from 1913 until his death in retirement. He had a long association with Louis Bleriot, famous for his pioneering flight across the English Channel in 1909. Chereau established a flying school at Hendon on Bleriot's behalf and opened a Bleriot aircraft factory at Brooklands in 1913, transferring the flying school there also. Another Bleriot facility, also managed by Chereau, began in Station Road, Addlestone, in 1916. It closed around 1922. Chereau's Addlestone home was The Hollies, Crockford Park Road. He is buried in Addlestone Cemetery with his wife, Maud Ellen Jane Chereau, née Hardy (1877-1949).

The men of Addlestone and the surrounding district who gave their lives in the Great War 1914-1918 and whose names are inscribed on the memorial gates of Victory Park

A recent photograph of the Memorial Gates, taken in early spring

A'COURT, Leonard Percy Frank

Private 22012, 6th Bn. Buffs (East Kent Regiment)
Born at Brooklands Farm, Weybridge, 18 August 1899
Baptised, 23 September 1899, St James', Weybridge
Only son of Frank and Cecilia Mary A'Court, née Haines, of Australian Cottages, New Haw (m.1893); nephew of George Henry Haines, also a fatal casualty
Killed in action, 23 May 1918, France, age 18
Cemetery: MAILLY WOOD CEMETERY, MAILLY-MAILLET, Somme, France

'As briefly mentioned in our last issue, Pte. Leonard Percy Frank A'Court, of the East Kent Regt., - only son of Mrs. A'Court, of Australian Cottages, Newhaw – was killed in France on May 22nd, the news reaching his mother on June 4th. The young fellow (he was only 18 years and 9 months old) joined up in October, 1917, and left for France as recently as April 28th. Prior to enlisting he had been employed by Mr. E. A. Burgess, baker and confectioner, for nearly three years. Mrs. A'Court has also received information that her husband is in a French hospital, but the nature of his illness is at present unknown. He has been in France serving with the Royal Engineers since October, 1915.

Sec.-Lieut. C. Reader has written to the bereaved mother: "I was very sorry indeed to lose your son, for although he had been in France but a few weeks he was a very promising young lad, full of courage, grit and determination. His death was very sudden, for he was asleep in his dug-out when a shell fell right on top of him, so he never had the slightest suffering. All the members of his platoon wish me to convey to you their deepest sympathy, for he was very popular."

Mrs A'Court wishes to thank all the kind and numerous friends, through this journal, for the sympathy extended to them in their great loss.' (The Surrey Herald, June 14, 1918)

ADAMS, Arthur John

Private 10935, 13th Bn. East Surrey Regiment
Born in Addlestone, 1892
Baptised, 5 February 1893, St Paul's, Addlestone
Son of Arthur John and Emma Adams (d.1914), of Chapel Park Road, Addlestone (1911 census)
Killed in action, 26 November 1917, France, during the Battle of Cambrai, age 25
Memorial: CAMBRAI MEMORIAL, LOUVERVAL, Nord, France

'Mr A. J. Adams, of the Princess Mary Village Homes, has now received an official intimation that owing to the lapse of time, his son – Pte. A. J. Adams, of the East Surrey Regiment – must be presumed to have been killed on November 26th 1917, the date upon which he was previously reported missing. The deceased joined the Forces on August 17th, 1914, and went out to France for the first time the following December. He had been wounded four times. Prior to enlisting, Pte. Adams was in the employ of Mowats Ltd., Weybridge.' (The Surrey Herald, November 1, 1918)

ADAMS, Stanley

Second Lieutenant, 9th Bn. Northumberland Fusiliers
Born in Kentish Town, 1887
Son of Aaron and Margaret Ellen Adams of Weybridge Road, Addlestone (1911 census);
husband of Jean Elizabeth Buss (formerly Adams), née Marchant, of "Gorselands",
Chesham Bois, Bucks. (m.1915)
Died of wounds, 9 September 1917, France, age 30
Cemetery: TEMPLEUX-LE-GUERARD COMMUNAL CEMETERY EXTENSION, Somme, France

ALLEN, Herbert

Lance Corporal 230549, 1/2nd (City of London) Bn. (Royal Fusiliers)
London Regiment
Born in Westminster, 1896
Eldest son of Herbert and Mary Allen, née Pyle, of "Kenilworth", Green Lane, Addlestone (m.1894)
Killed in action, 16 August 1917, Belgium, during the Battle of Langemarck, part of the Third Battle of Ypres (Passchendaele), age 21
Memorial: YPRES (MENIN GATE) MEMORIAL, Ieper, West-Vlaanderen, Belgium

'Lc.-Cpl. Allen is the elder son of Mr. and Mrs. H. Allen, of Kenilworth, Green-lane, Addlestone. He joined the Forces in September, 1914, and within two days was on his way to Malta. After a period of three months training at the Mediterranean island he was transferred to France, and, almost immediately, was sent to the firing line.

As already mentioned in "The Herald", he received two Distinguished Service Cards for gallant conduct in the field. Although he took part in some of the fiercest fighting he remained unscathed, and was at home on leave in the early part of the year. The officer commanding the Company states that Lc.-Cpl. Allen was last seen as the troops went into action on Aug. 16th.' (The Surrey Herald, October 12, 1917)

ALLEN, William

Details unknown

AUSTIN, Ronald Grantham

Lance Corporal STK/221, 10th Bn. Royal Fusiliers (City of London Regiment)
Born in Romford, 1884
Son of George and Caroline Austin, née Breckels, of Brighton Road, Addlestone (m.1879)
Killed in action, 23 April 1917, France, during the Arras Offensive and the Second Battle of the Scarpe, age 33
Cemetery: CHILI TRENCH CEMETERY, GAVRELLE, Pas de Calais, France

'Much sympathy will be extended to Mr. and Mrs. George Austin, of Elba Villa, Liberty-lane, who on Monday received the official news that their second son, Cpl. Ronald Grantham Austin, of the Royal Fusiliers, had been killed in France on the 23rd April.

The deceased N.C.O., who was in his 33rd year, joined up on the outbreak of war, leaving his berth at the London Stock Exchange. Up to the time of his death he had served in France for 22 months, and had emerged from several large battles, the last of which was the Vimy Ridge.

The late Cpl. Austin was well known in Addlestone, where he took a keen interest in sport. The parents have one other son serving in France with the London Rifle Brigade.'
(The Surrey Herald, May 25, 1917)

AWCOCK, Frederick Charles

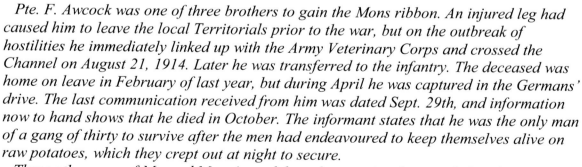

Private 42020, 5th Bn. North Staffordshire Regiment
Born in Addlestone, 1893
Son of Peter Robert and Jane Awcock, née Newman, of York Villas, Chertsey Road, Addlestone (m.1893)
Died, 24 October 1918, POW in Germany, age 24
Cemetery: SARRALBE MILITARY CEMETERY, Moselle, France

'Through a returned prisoner-of-war Mr. and Mrs. Peter Awcock, of York Villa, Addlestone Moor, have learned that their second son, Pte. Fred Awcock, of the 5th North Staffords, died from starvation whilst a prisoner with the Germans.

Pte. F. Awcock was one of three brothers to gain the Mons ribbon. An injured leg had caused him to leave the local Territorials prior to the war, but on the outbreak of hostilities he immediately linked up with the Army Veterinary Corps and crossed the Channel on August 21, 1914. Later he was transferred to the infantry. The deceased was home on leave in February of last year, but during April he was captured in the Germans' drive. The last communication received from him was dated Sept. 29th, and information now to hand shows that he died in October. The informant states that he was the only man of a gang of thirty to survive after the men had endeavoured to keep themselves alive on raw potatoes, which they crept out at night to secure.

Three other sons of Mr. and Mrs. Awcock have been seriously wounded in the war. Pte. Albert Awcock, who was in the 1st East Surreys at Mons, secured his discharge after being hit by a bullet in the right hand whilst fighting in Serbia. Pte. R. Awcock, who was also in the 1st East Surreys at Mons, is still lying in the Brooklands (Weybridge) hospital after being hit in the leg by a bullet ten months ago; and Pte. E. Awcock, of the 4th Norfolks, had his hip smashed by a bullet 15 months since, and is now in a hospital at Bethnal Green.

The four daughters of Mr. and Mrs. Awcock were all in munitions works.' (The Surrey Herald, February 7, 1919)

AYRES, Henry

Private 34939, 2nd Bn. Leicestershire Regiment
Born in Stratfield Saye, Hampshire, 29 July 1882
Son of Neptune and Athalia Ayres, née Gregory (d.1912) of Common Lane, New Haw;
husband of Louisa Ayres, née Harris, of Meads Lane, Chertsey (m.1901)
Killed in action, 9 March 1917, Mesopotamia, during the advance on Baghdad (occupied
by British forces 11 March 1917), age 35
Memorial: BASRA MEMORIAL, Iraq

*'Mrs. Ayres, of Rowhill, has learned that her husband, Pte. H. Ayres, of the Leicester
Regt., was killed in Mesopotamia during March. Pte. Ayres was a brick-maker in the
employ of Messrs. Roake, Hatch Farm, when war was declared, and he enlisted soon
afterwards. About a couple of years since he left this country for overseas. The deceased,
who was 36 years of age, leaves a widow and four children.' (The Surrey Herald, May
25, 1917)*

BAILEY, George Alfred William

Lance Corporal 10735, A Coy. 5th Bn. Royal Berkshire Regiment
Born in Addlestone, 1894
Baptised, 10 June 1894, St Paul's, Addlestone
Son of Charles and Ellen Bailey, née Paulley, of Marsh Lane,
Addlestone (m.1882)
Died, 24 October 1915, 3rd General Hospital, Le Treport, France, age 21
Cemetery: LE TREPORT MILITARY CEMETERY, Seine-Maritime,
France

*'The sad news has been received by Mr. and Mrs. C. Bailey, of Marsh Lane,
Addlestone, that their third son, Corpl. G. Bailey, of the 5th Berkshire Regt., has
succumbed to wounds to his head in the 3rd General Hospital, Le Trepart, France.
Wounded in the recent battle of Loos, he passed peacefully away last Sunday.*

*Corpl. Bailey, who joined up in the first month of the war, was at one time gardener at
"Rivermead", Addlestone.' (The Surrey Herald, October 29, 1915)*

BARTRAM, James Edward

Private 7562, 7th Bn. East Surrey Regiment
Enlisted, 6 August 1914
Born in Addlestone, 1896
Son of James Edward (d.1904) and Frances Mary Bartram, née Mathewes, of Windsor
Street, Chertsey (m.1896); cousin of George and Percival Cranston, also fatal casualties
Killed in action, 13 August 1916, France, during the Battle of the Somme, age 20
Cemetery: POZIERES BRITISH CEMETERY, OVILLERS-LA BOISSELLE, Somme,
France

*'I believe we were insane at the time. My wound is in the muscle of my right arm – only
a burst an inch deep. I received it near the Hulluch Quarry, near Loos, and a warm place
it is. Eastleigh is a nice place; we are getting very good food here and lots of it and –
spring beds! Everything for comfort and we are very thankful for it. I have the German
helmet still.' (The Surrey Herald, October 15, 1915 - written on a postcard to his mother
while being treated in Devon for wounds received at the Battle of Loos in 1915)*

BASSON, Harry William

Driver 26589, Royal Field Artillery
Born in Addlestone, 1880
Son of Edward W. (d.1910) and Mary Basson, of Simplemarsh Road, Addlestone
(1911 census); husband of Maude Basson, née Beauchamp, of Simplemarsh Road,
Addlestone (m.1907)
Died, 25 November 1916, France, age 36
Cemetery: STE. MARIE CEMETERY, LE HAVRE, Seine-Maritime, France

'Yet another Addlestone soldier has made the supreme sacrifice in France, in the person of Driver Harry William Basson, of the Royal Field Artillery, whose wife and family reside in Simplemarsh-road.

Mrs Basson received a War Office statement on Thursday last, stating that her husband had succumbed on the 25th November, death being due to valvular disease of the heart. It is believed that he passed away quite suddenly.

The deceased soldier, who was on the Reserve, was called up on the 5th August, 1914, and about three weeks later he was sent across to France, where he had served until the time of his death. Prior to being called up he was employed as under-gardener at Oakley Lodge, Addlestone. Driver Basson, who was 35 years of age, leaves a wife and four children to mourn their loss.' (The Surrey Herald, December 8, 1916)

BATCHELOR, Frederick Edward

Private G/7549, B Coy. 7th Bn. Queen's (Royal West Surrey Regiment)
Born in Oatlands Park, Weybridge, 1890
Son of Frederick and Sarah Batchelor, née Keyte (d.1916), of Courland
Lodge, Chertsey Road, Addlestone
Died of wounds, 5 April 1918, France, age 28
Cemetery: ST. SEVER CEMETERY EXTENSION, ROUEN, Seine-
Maritime, France

'News has been received by Mr. F. Batchelor, of Addlestone Hill, that his eldest son, Pte. F. E. Batchelor, of The Queen's, has died of wounds. Pte. Batchelor passed away in the Australian Hospital, Rouen, as the result of wounds received by the bursting of a shell on April 4th. He served in the local Territorials, but he was unable to go abroad with them as he was unfit. He enlisted in 1916, prior to which he was employed as a gardener at Englefield Green. Mr. Batchelor received the sad news from the Major of the hospital.

Another son of Mr. Batchelor's, Lc.-Cpl. G. Batchelor, of the East Surreys, has been wounded in the arm and is now lying in the 1st General Hospital, Etreat, France. Lc. Cpl. Batchelor enlisted on the outbreak of war and he has been previously gassed, and twice wounded. He was formerly employed at Simplemarsh Farm.' (The Surrey Herald, April 19, 1918)

BAVIN, William Joseph

Lance Corporal 4045, 23rd Bn. Royal Fusiliers (City of London
Regiment)
Born in Croydon, 1882
Only son of Joseph Ashby and Annie Bavin, née Tucknott, of Rydings
Cottage, Liberty Lane, Addlestone (m.1879)
Killed in action, 30 January 1917, France, age 35
Cemetery: COURCELETTE BRITISH CEMETERY, Somme, France

'We regret having to record the death of yet another Addlestone soldier in the person of Lc.-Cpl. William Joseph Bavin of the Royal Fusiliers, the only son of Mr. and Mrs. Bavin, of Ryding Cottage, Liberty Lane.

The following is an extract from a letter recently received by the parents from a Lieutenant of the Regiment. "It is my painful duty to write and tell you of the death of your son in action, and I wish to offer you my very sincere sympathy in your sad loss. He was killed by a shell or trench mortar, which wounded two others, on Sunday night, Jan. 30th. Death was instantaneous, and caused by concussion, as there was not a wound visible. No doubt it will relieve you considerably to know that he had a decent burial the following night, a number of miles behind the line, in a Brigade cemetery, where rest a number of other brave comrades who have "done their bit."

The late Lc.-Cpl. Bavin, who was 34 years of age, had seen about 12 months fighting in France. He enlisted in June 1915, joining the Sportsmen's Battalion, and was later transferred to the Royal Fusiliers. Prior to joining the Forces the deceased was employed at Messrs. Coatman & Sons, at Haslemere.' (The Surrey Herald, February 23, 1917)

BAXTER, Charles

Private 75371, 13th Bn. Royal Fusiliers (City of London Regiment)
Born in Lyne, 1879
3rd son of James (d.1918) and Elizabeth Baxter; husband of Anne Matilda Baxter, née Coe, of New Haw Farm, Addlestone (m.1899)
Killed in action, 5 April 1918, France, near Bucquoy, on the final day of the German Spring Offensive, age 38
Memorial: ARRAS MEMORIAL, Pas de Calais, France

BEAUMONT, Sydney David

Rifleman 322766, 1/6th (City of London) Bn. (Rifles) London Regiment
Born in Edgware, 1889
Son of David and Elizabeth Beaumont, of Edgware; husband of Agnes M Beaumont, née Grant, of Milton House, Addlestone (m.1911).
Daughter, Joan Grant Beaumont, died June 1915, age 7 weeks
Killed in action, 22 October 1916, France, during the Battle of the Somme, age 26
Memorial: YPRES (MENIN GATE) MEMORIAL, Ieper, West-Vlaanderen, Belgium

'Mrs. Beaumont, newsagent and stationer, of Station Gates has recently received further news regarding the fate of her husband, Rifleman S.D. Beaumont, of the City of London Regt., who was recently reported in our columns as "missing" after being but ten days in France. Two letters have been received by his wife, one from the Lieutenant of his company and the other from a comrade. Both writers entertain very little hope that he is alive, and the former states that there was a large mine explosion on the day specified – the 22nd of October.' (The Surrey Herald, December 8, 1916)

BOLTON, Philip Leslie Alfred

Private 31010, No. 2 Coy. New Zealand Machine Gun Corps
Born in Addlestone, 1896
Baptised, 3 May 1896, St Paul's, Addlestone
Son of Granville Edward William (b.1873, Addlestone) and Georgina Bolton, née
Curgenven, of Seddon Road, Hamilton West Waikato, New Zealand (m.1894)
Family sailed from London, 26 June 1914, to New Zealand on SS Athenic
Died, 4 October 1917, Belgium, during the 3rd Battle of Ypres (Passchendaele), age 21
Memorial: TYNE COT MEMORIAL, Zonnebeke, West-Vlaanderen, Belgium

BOVINGTON, Alfred George

Private 40215, 1/4th Bn. Leicestershire Regiment
Born in Addlestone, 1891
Baptised, 20 May 1891, St Paul's, Addlestone
Son of George and Alice Annie Bovington, née Whattingham, of
Garfield Cottages, Addlestone
Killed in action, 16 August 1918, France, age 27
Cemetery: FOUQUIERES CHURCHYARD EXTENSION, Pas de
Calais, France

'Mr. and Mrs. G. Bovington, of 4, Garfield Cottages, have learned that
their eldest son, Pte. Alfred Bovington, Leicestershire Regt., was killed in France during
August. He enlisted nearly three years ago – prior to which he was in the employ of Mr.
Gayland, carman, Byfleet – and two years ago was seriously wounded during the Somme
fighting.
     Among letters received by the parents have been the following:- Capt. Frank Brown: " I
cannot tell you how much he will be missed by all in the Company. He was one of the best
workers I have." The Rev. R. K. Davis (Chaplain): "Your son was killed by a shell, and
buried by me in Tonquieres cemetery. A cross is being placed over the grave, which will
be well looked after. He died as a soldier and for the sake of his friends." A comrade, Pte.
A. P. Cox: "Pte. Bovington was killed instantaneously as a shell dropped at his feet,
killing two men and wounding three. All the boys in his platoon will miss him, as he was
always jolly and bright." (The Surrey Herald, September 6, 1918)

BRYAN, Norman Ford

Ordinary Seaman J/22422, H.M.S. *Monmouth*, Royal Navy
Born in Addlestone, 1896
Elder son of James and Annie Eleanor Bryan, née Ford, of High
Street, Addlestone (m.1893)
Died, 1 November 1914, on H.M.S. *Monmouth*, age 18

H.M.S. *Monmouth*, an armoured cruiser of 9,950 tons, commissioned
in 1903, was sunk by gunfire on 1 November 1914 by German
armoured cruisers off the Chilean Coast during the Battle of Coronel.
H.M.S. *Good Hope* was also sunk. There were no survivors among
the two crews, totalling about 1,600.
Memorial: CHATHAM NAVAL MEMORIAL, Kent, United Kingdom

'On board the "Monmouth" – which figured in the fight off the Chilean coast – was a
smart young Addlestone sailor in Norman Bryan, of High Street. Joining the Navy a
couple of years ago, young Bryan made unusually good progress, as in shooting he
headed the sixty boys on his training ship, the "Royal Arthur", and was rated A.B. at the

early age of 17½, or six months younger than the average sailor. He was transferred to the "Monmouth" on the outbreak of war, as previously he had been on the Falmouth, which for some months was off the Irish coast with the gun running incidents. Bryan was but 18 years of age the day before the fight – Sunday week – in which his boat is believed to have foundered, and all hands lost.' (The Surrey Herald, November 13, 1914)

BURGESS, Lawrence Francis

Private 2484, Surrey Yeomanry (Queen Mary's Regiment)
Born in Slough, 1886
Son of Edward and Alice Burgess; husband of Ethel Leigh Burgess, née Vickery, of Albert Road, Addlestone (m.1907)
Captain of Chertsey Cricket Club; member of St. Augustine's Church choir
Died, 26 January 1915, Surrey County Hospital, Guildford, age 28
Cemetery: ADDLESTONE BURIAL GROUND, Surrey, United Kingdom

'Many young sportsmen throughout the neighbourhood of Addlestone and Chertsey will learn with keen regret of the death of Mr. Lawrence Francis ('Laurie') Burgess, youngest son of Mr. Edward Burgess, who recently moved to Weybridge after a lengthy sojourn in Addlestone.

Less than three weeks ago 'Laurie' Burgess – as he was popularly known – visited Addlestone, looking the picture of health in his khaki uniform. Just previously to Christmas he had enlisted in the Surrey (Queen Mary's) Yeomanry and there was no doubt that the new life was suitable to the young sportsman. Soon after arriving back in camp, however, appendicitis made its presence evident, and he was conveyed from the camp at Dorking by motor to the Surrey County Hospital at Guildford. There he underwent operations on January 15th and 22nd, but he gradually sank until his death on Tuesday, at the early age of 28.

The deceased leaves a widow (the daughter of Mr. and Mrs. H. L. Vickery, of Chertsey), and two young children, who have recently been staying at the house of Mr Burgess, senior, in Minorca Road, Weybridge.' (The Surrey Herald, January 29, 1915)

BUTLER, Vincent Mark

Gunner 74115, 67th Siege Bty. Royal Garrison Artillery
Born in Spratts, Ottershaw, 1893
Baptised, 26 March 1893, St Paul's, Addlestone
Son of Mark and Annie Butler, of Ottershaw; husband of Helena C. Butler, née Bates, of Chobham Road, Ottershaw (m.1913)
Died, 16 October 1917, France, from wounds received from shell-fire, age 24
Cemetery: GODEWAERSVELDE BRITISH CEMETERY, Nord, France

'Much sympathy has been extended to Nurse and Mr. Butler, of Spratts, who have recently sustained a great bereavement by the death from wounds in France of their eldest son, Gunner V. Butler, of the Royal Garrison Artillery.

The deceased's wife, who also resides in Ottershaw, has received the official War Office notification, in addition to letters from his officer, nurse and comrades. The deceased Gunner was 24 years of age, and well known in the district, being a postman at Ottershaw prior to enlisting in April of 1916. He crossed to France the following August. It was only about three weeks previous to his death that the deceased was home enjoying a brief respite from the Front.

Major L. Taylor has written: "I am extremely sorry to be the writer of sad news for you. Your poor husband was wounded on the 12th October by a shell. He was taken straight to the hospital, but he was not able to survive the shock. The poor fellow died on the 16th and was buried in the hospital cemetery. Everything that could be done to save him was done, but it was willed that he should pay the supreme sacrifice. He did his duty well and cheerfully, and the whole Battery is sorry to lose him. On their behalf I ask you to accept my sincerest sympathy with you in your cruel bereavement."

The Sister-in-charge of the casualty clearing station has written as follows: "Your husband was brought in here very badly wounded in the left arm and thigh, and though we did all we possibly could to save him I am sorry to say it was of no use, and he passed away at 3.20 this afternoon. At least he died in comfort and among friends. He sent his love, and to tell you of the wounds, but he was too ill to talk much."

The following is an extract from the comrade's letter: "We were all deeply grieved to hear of his death, for we all thought that he was just hurt enough to get home with it. He was just getting something out of his pocket at the time, close to the gun, when a shell came over, and he was hit with a splinter. We put him on a stretcher and carried him about 100 yards to the dressing station, and he was dressed right away, and we thought that also was in his favour, but it seems that fate was against him and you know the rest. He was one of our best workers, and was very much liked by all his section." (The Surrey Herald, November 9, 1917)

CHALCRAFT, Arthur

Sapper 37113, 68th Field Coy. Corps of Royal Engineers
Born in Addlestone, 1892
Baptised, 27 March 1892, St Paul's, Addlestone
Son of William and Emily Chalcraft; husband of Olive A. Chalcraft, née Whattingham (m.1914)
Killed in action, 26 September 1916, France, during the Battle of the Somme, aged 24
Cemetery: OVILLERS MILITARY CEMETERY, Somme, France

'We regret having to record the death of another Addlestonian on the field of honour in Sapper H. Chalcraft, the youngest son of Mr. and Mrs. Chalcraft, of Albert-road.

The deceased soldier enlisted in May, 1915, joining the Royal Engineers. The following November he was sent to Egypt, where he remained until July of the present year, when he was transferred to France. He was 24 years of age, and prior to joining the Forces he kept a boot repairing business in Addlestone.

Sapper Chalcraft leaves a wife and one child to mourn their loss. His wife, who is at present residing with her mother in Portmore Park, Weybridge, received the following letter on October 4th from the Section Officer:- "It is with the greatest regret that I write to inform you of the circumstances of your husband's death on the afternoon of the 29th September. He was moving up with the rest of my section when he was hit by a piece of shell in the left side. He remained practically unconscious until the time of his death, which occurred about 10 minutes later. Two of his comrades remained with him until the end. Will you please accept our very deepest sympathy in your irreparable loss? In some small way we can appreciate how much this bereavement must mean to you, as your husband was liked by all who knew him, and in addition was one of our best and most reliable men.' (The Surrey Herald, October 13, 1916)

CHANDLER, Harry Evans

Private CH/588(S), Chatham Bn. Royal Naval Division
Enlisted, 29 December 1914
Born in Addlestone, 17 January 1892
Baptised, 10 April 1892, St Paul's, Addlestone
Son of William and Mary Ann Chandler, née Hatton, of Ecton Road,
Addlestone (1911 census) (m.1888)
Killed in action, 2 September 1915, Turkey, Gallipoli Peninsula, age
23
Memorial: HELLES MEMORIAL, Turkey

‘The sad news reached Mr. and Mrs. Chandler, of "The Bungalow", Liberty Lane on Monday morning, that their second son, Pte. Harry Evans Chandler, of the Royal Marine Light Infantry, had been killed in action on the Gallipoli Peninsula.

For several years the deceased was an auxiliary postman attached to the Addlestone staff, and the reason he did not don khaki prior to December 28th was solely due to the fact that he wanted to secure a position on the staff. That position attained, he joined up with the Chatham Battalion of the Royal Naval Division (R.M.L.I.)

The official notification stated that Pte. Chandler was killed on September 2nd. The news, as stated, arrived on Monday, only two days previously to which Mr. and Mrs. Chandler had received a very cheerful letter from their son, who therein referred to the fact that so far he had come unscathed through several engagements.' (The Surrey Herald, September 17, 1915)

CHANDLER, William Stanley

Corporal 10078, 7th Bn. East Surrey Regiment
Enlisted, 25 October 1910
Born in Addlestone, 1892
Son of James Henry (d.1908) and Alice Chandler, née Marsh, of
Common Lane, New Haw, Addlestone (1911 census) (m.1893)
Killed in action, 9 April 1917, France, on the first day of the Battle of
Arras, age 25
Cemetery: CABARET-ROUGE BRITISH CEMETERY, SOUCHEZ,
Pas de Calais, France

‘Many expressions of sympathy have been extended to Mrs. Chandler, of Common-lane, New Haw, who has recently received the news of the death in France of her eldest son, Cpl. William Stanley Chandler, of the East Surrey Regt.

The intimation, which was received by Mrs. Chandler during last week, took the form of two letters, one from the Officer Commanding and the other from a comrade. Both letters spoke in very high terms of the late Cpl. Chandler, the officer stating that the deceased would have been made a Sergeant had he pulled through the battle which took place on the 9th April.

The comrade, in writing to the mother, stated that they attacked on the 9th April, and Cpl. Chandler was one of the most cheerful of the whole platoon. When they reached the first German lines he was hit by a bullet, and the platoon passed on to the sixth German line. Cpl. Chandler was "one of the best" in every respect.

The deceased N.C.O., who was 25 years of age, enlisted in November, 1912. He was drafted to India soon after entering the Army, but shortly after the outbreak of war the Regiment was transferred to France. The deceased had been in France but a few weeks when he contracted frozen feet. He was brought home to England, and did not return until January, 1916.

Mrs. Chandler has four other sons serving their King and country, two each in the Navy and Army.' (The Surrey Herald, May 4, 1917)

CHATFIELD, Charles John

Private 32948, 12th Bn. East Surrey Regiment
Born in Norwood, 1883
Son of Arthur and Emma Chatfield, of Norwood; husband of Hilda Mary Chatfield, née Curwood, of High Street, Addlestone (m.1915)
Killed in action, 3 September 1918, Belgium, during The Advance in Flanders, age 35
Cemetery: KLEIN-VIERSTRAAT BRITISH CEMETERY, Heuvelland, West-Vlaanderen, Belgium

'Many friends and acquaintances have learned with deep regret that Lc.-Cpl. C. J. Chatfield, of the East Surrey Regt., was killed in action on Sept. 3rd. Until his enlistment about two years ago the deceased was the collector to the West Surrey Water Co., and in his absence the work has been continued by his wife, who learned the sad tidings on Tuesday.

Lc.-Cpl. Chatfield, who had declined an invitation to train for a commission, arrived home from France as recently as August 4th, and he did not return until August 17th. He wrote to his wife on Sept. 2nd, and the letter reached her just prior to another, from his platoon officer, announcing his death. The deceased was 35 years of age.' (The Surrey Herald, September 13, 1918)

CLARK, William John

Corporal 10897, 5th Bn. Dorsetshire Regiment
Born in Haslemere, 17 March 1894
Son of George Arthur and Clara Clark, née White, of Basingstoke Cottages, Common Lane, New Haw (m.1893)
Killed in action, 26 September 1916, France, while taking part in an attack near Mouquet Farm, during the Battle of the Somme, age 22
Memorial: THIEPVAL MEMORIAL, Somme, France

'During November of last year we reported that Cpl. W.J. Clark, of the 5th Dorsets, had been officially reported as missing after an engagement on the 26th Sept. 1916. Mr. and Mrs. Clark, who reside at No. 8 Basingstoke Cottages, New Haw, have now received the official news from the War Office that their son must have been killed in action on that date.

The deceased was the eldest son, and 20 years of age. He enlisted in September, 1914, and served throughout the Dardanelles campaign. He also saw considerable service in Egypt, and was in France only four months when he was reported missing. Prior to joining the Forces the deceased was employed as a gardener at "The Cedars" Addlestone. The parents' other son, who is attached to the K.R.R's, is still in hospital having been wounded last September.' (The Surrey Herald, June 29, 1917)

COLE, William John
Private G/6242, 10th Bn. Queen's (Royal West Surrey Regiment)
Born in Pyrford, 27 August 1878
Son of John and Mary Jane Cole, née White, of New Haw Road, New Haw (1901 census)
Killed in action, 15 September 1916, France, near Flers, during the Battle of the Somme, age 38
Memorial: THIEPVAL MEMORIAL, Somme, France

COLLIER, Robert Gordon

Private 42292, 2nd Bn. Royal Inniskilling Fusiliers
Born in Addlestone, 1890
Son of James and Evelyn Collier, of Lime Grove, Addlestone; husband of Daisy Maud Collier, née Harris, of Primrose Cottages, Addlestone Moor (m.1914)
Killed in action, 3 December 1917, Belgium, age 26
Memorial: TYNE COT MEMORIAL, Zonnebeke, West-Vlaanderen, Belgium

   'Mr J. Collier, of 7 Lime Grove, Church-road, would greatly appreciate any tidings concerning his son – Pte. Robert Collier, of the Inniskilling Fusiliers, who has been missing since Dec. 3, 1917. The parents have lived in Addlestone for over 20 years, and consequently the missing soldier, who joined H.M. Forces 2½ years ago, was well known locally. Any information that may lead to details concerning his last being seen or heard of will be thankfully received at the above address. Mr. Collier has three other sons serving with the Colours overseas' (The Surrey Herald, May 10, 1918)

COOPER, Albert Isaac

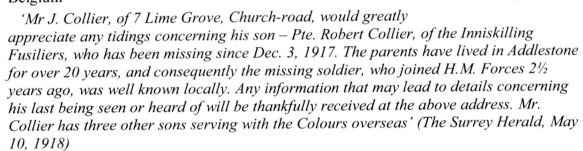

Private 202564, 4th Bn. Gordon Highlanders
Born in Shepperton, 1897
Second son of Alfred John (d.1907) and Edith Sarah Cooper, née Flippance, of Liberty Hall Road, Addlestone (m.1895)
Killed in action, 9 April 1917, France, on the first day of the Battle of Arras, age 19
Cemetery: ROCLINCOURT VALLEY CEMETERY, Pas de Calais, France

   'It is with the very deepest regret that we record to-day the death in France of two Addlestone soldier brothers, Pte. A. W. Cooper, of the Gordon Highlanders, and Pte. A. I. Cooper, also of the Gordon Highlanders, the two sons of Mrs. Cooper, a widow, residing in Liberty Hall-road.
   During the latter end of last week Mrs. Cooper received a letter from the matron of a casualty clearing station, which read as follows: "Pte. A. Cooper was admitted to this station very badly wounded. He only lived a few hours, and I am afraid I have no message for you, but I thought it might comfort you a little to know he was gently laid to rest and buried in the cemetery, and his grave marked with a cross."
   By this letter Mrs. Cooper could not tell which of her sons had fallen, as the letter only mentioned the first initial, and gave no number. But yesterday morning (Thursday) another letter was received, from the Chaplain to the Forces, the following of which is an extract: "I regret very much to write you about the death of your son, 6071, Pte. A. I. Cooper. He was killed in action on the 9th April in the great battle which commenced on

that day. He was buried on the field of battle, with some of his comrades, in a spot which they had gained from the enemy. Your boy did well – served his Battalion nobly, and he is mourned and missed by all his comrades. Please accept my deep sympathy."

This letter was a terrible blow to Mrs. Cooper, who knew that not only had one of her sons fallen – but both had made the supreme sacrifice.

Pte. A. W. Cooper was the eldest son, and 21 years of age. He enlisted in February of 1916, and crossed to France in July of the same year. For many years he was employed as a gardener at "Coombelands", Addlestone.

Pte. A. I. Cooper was the second son, and only 19 years of age. He left for France last November, having enlisted in August, 1916. For three years he was in the gardens at "The Cedars", and later was employed at the St. George's College.' (The Surrey Herald, April 27, 1917)

COOPER, Alfred William

Private S/11453, D Coy. 1st Bn. Gordon Highlanders
Born in Chertsey, 1896
Elder son of Alfred John (d.1907) and Edith Sarah Cooper, née Flippance, of Liberty Hall Road, Addlestone (m.1895)
Died, 10 April 1917, France, from wounds received on the first day of the Battle of Arras, age 21
Cemetery: DUISANS BRITISH CEMETERY, ETRUN, Pas de Calais, France

COOPER, Gilbert Noel

Driver 81017, Royal Field Artillery
Born in Weybridge, 4 August 1897
Son of Charles and Eliza Cooper, née Hursey, of Victoria Road, Addlestone (m.1890)
Died of wounds, 23 April 1918, France, age 20
Cemetery: LAPUGNOY MILITARY CEMETERY, Pas de Calais, France

'Information reached the parents on Sunday of the death from wounds of Bomb. Gilbert Noel Cooper, R.F.A., the son of Mr. and Mrs. Chas. Cooper, of Victoria-road. He had succumbed on April 23rd. Bomb. Cooper's 17th birthday was on the day that war was declared, and he joined up a few days afterwards. Prior to enlisting he was second gardener to Sir John Kemp, of Oakwood, Weybridge. The deceased had been in France two years next August.' (The Surrey Herald, May 10, 1918)

COTTON, William Alfred

Private, Royal Scots Fusiliers
Born in Addlestone, 1890
Son of John and Sarah Cotton, née Palmer, of Victoria Road, Addlestone (1901 census) (m.1882)
Killed in action, 12 October 1916, France, age 25
Memorial: UNKNOWN

'Unofficial intimation has been received by Mrs. Cowlard, of Mathew

Cottages, Westfield, Woking, of the death of her brother, Pte. Wm. Alfred Cotton, whose parents reside at 53, Victoria-road, Addlestone. He was a son of Sergt. J. Cotton, of the Rifle Brigade, and prior to the outbreak of war was employed in some motor works at Weybridge. After being trained in Scotland he went out with his Regiment, the Royal Scots Fusiliers, in the early autumn of last year, and just before his death was acting as leading gunner in the Lewis Machine Gun Corps.

The sad news was conveyed in a letter from a chum (Lc.-Cpl. Dennie), who wrote that Pte. Cotton was killed on Oct. 12. Describing how it occurred, he says: "The section had just returned from a successful charge, and we had got back into the trenches. Your brother and I were sitting together, when I got word to go further up the trench. When I got back, within a few minutes, I found your brother had been killed. He was a good soldier and well liked by us all. We were able to give him a decent burial, and erect a little wooden cross. The men miss him greatly, as he was a good pal. He died a soldier's death, fighting for his King, country and the folks he loved at home. I would have written before only I was wounded immediately afterwards, but am all right again."

Mrs. Cowlard is the wife of one of the band of eight Cowlard brothers who are at the Front, her husband serving with the A.S.C. Remounts.

Since writing the above official news has been received from the War Office of Pte. Cotton's death. It is just two years ago since a son-in-law of Mr. Cotton (Pte. H. Green, of Woking and the Royal Sussex) was killed at Mons. Mr. Cotton has only one son left now, and he is serving in the Army with the A.S.C.' (The Surrey Herald, December 15, 1916)

COX, Valentine
Boy 1st Class, H.M.S. *Stephen Furness*
Enlisted, 23 July 1915
Born in Addlestone, 14 February 1900
Son of James Henry and Florence Ellen Cox, née Barrett (d.1906), of Liberty Hall Road, Addlestone (m.1898)
Died, 13 December 1917, on H.M.S. *Stephen Furness*, aged 17

H.M.S. *Stephen Furness*, an armed boarding steamer of 1,712 tons, was torpedoed by a German submarine in the Irish Sea. The ship sank with the loss of 101 officers and men.
Memorial: CHATHAM NAVAL MEMORIAL, Kent, United Kingdom

CRANSTON, George
Lance Sergeant 10368, 9th Bn. East Surrey Regiment
Enlisted, 16 January 1912
Born in Addlestone, 1893
Son of George (d.1919) and Florence Mary Cranston, née Hopley, of Belle Vue, Hare Hill (m.1886); cousin of James Edward Bartram, also a fatal casualty
Killed in action, 27 March 1918, France, during the German Spring Offensive, age 25
Memorial: POZIERES MEMORIAL, Somme, France

'Reference was made in our last issue to the fact that Pte.Cranston, of the East Surreys, and Hare Hill, Ottershaw, had been wounded for the fourth time.

His father has now learned that he is in the Edinburgh Hospital, Bangor (Scotland), suffering from wounds in the head, right hand, and each leg.

On the first occasion Pte. G. Cranston (reference to whose good work with the bombs appears on page 5 of to-day's issue) was in Netley Hospital, with a wound in his left elbow; later he was a patient at Ampton Hall, Bury St. Edmunds, with frozen feet. On again reaching the trenches he was wounded in the leg, to recover in the base hospital at Havre, and on the next occasion, when his shoulder was slightly injured, a field dressing sufficed.

Private P. Cranston, a brother, was killed last November, and a younger brother, Leslie, is in France, with the machine gun section of the 7th West Surreys.' (The Surrey Herald, October 15, 1915)

'Mr. and Mrs. Cranston, of Belle Vue, Hare Hill, have received telegraphic information that one of their sons, Pte. Arthur Cranston, of the Royal West Kents, was wounded in the thigh on the 22nd Sept. He is progressing favourably, and has been transferred to a base hospital. Mr. Cranston wishes to contradict a rumour that his son, Sergt. G. Cranston, is known to be a prisoner of war. No information to this effect has come to hand. He has been missing since March 24th, and any information regarding him will be gratefully received by the parents. Another son, Pte. F. Cranston, has returned to France after recovering from wounds.' (The Surrey Herald, October 4, 1918)

CRANSTON, Percival

Private 9922, 2nd Bn. Queen's (Royal West Surrey Regiment)
Enlisted, 4 July 1911
Born in Addlestone, 1890
Baptised, 4 January 1891, Christchurch, Ottershaw
Son of George (d.1919) and Florence Mary Cranston, née Hopley, of Belle Vue, Hare Hill (m.1886); cousin of James Edward Bartram, also a fatal casualty
Died of wounds, 7 November 1914, No.4 Clearing Hospital, Poperinghe, age 24
Cemetery: POPERINGHE OLD MILITARY CEMETERY, Poperinghe, West-Vlaanderen, Belgium

'Pte. Percy Cranston, 2nd R.W.S. (Queen's) Regiment, who was a son of Mr. and Mrs. George Cranston, of Belle Vue, Hare Hill, Ottershaw, has been killed in action. The notification only reached his parents on Monday, a month after he was killed in France. Aged 24, he was in South Africa with his Regiment in August, having been in the Army for five years. The last card received from him stated that he was feeling fit and well.

As soon as the news was known at Addlestone St. Paul's School, the headmaster sent a letter of sympathy to the mother, hoping that the noble manner of his death would be some consolation. The flag at the school was strung at half-mast.

Before joining the Army, Cranston was in the employ of the late Mr. R. H. Otter and of Mr. Gosling. He tried several times to enter the Services before he was accepted. Another son of Mr. Cranston, in the East Surreys, has been wounded, but is now back at the Front.' (The Surrey Herald, December 11, 1914)

'Pte. Percy Cranston, of the Queen's R.W.S. Regt., was killed near Ypres in 1914, after having spent three years in South Africa and without having had the opportunity of visiting his home prior to crossing to France.' (The Surrey Herald, July 6, 1917)

CROFT, Victor Sydney

Private 353414, 1/7th (City of London) Bn. London Regiment
Born in Chertsey, 1897
Son of George Robert Croft of Hughenden Villas, Addlestone and the
late Jane Croft, née Squelch (d.1906) (m.1892)
Killed in action, 7 October 1916, France, during the Battle of the
Somme, age 19
Cemetery: WARLENCOURT BRITISH CEMETERY, Pas de Calais,
France

'Information arrived on Sunday morning that Pte. Victor S. Croft, second son of Mr. G. Croft, of Hughenden Villas, Addlestone Moor, had been returned as missing after an engagement on Oct. 7th.

Pte. Victor Croft was formerly in the 2/6th East Surreys, but he was transferred to the City of London Regt. and had been in France only about two months. Before enlisting he was an apprentice with Messrs. Taylor and Bates, Bridge Wharf, Chertsey, and also a member of All Saints' Choir, Chertsey. He is only 19 years of age. His elder brother, Sergt. Inst. A. Croft, has been discharged from the Army in consequence of the wounds to his left arm in the first battle of La Bassee.' (The Surrey Herald, November 3, 1916)

DEADMAN, Frank William P

Lance Corporal L/10721, 2nd Bn. Queen's (Royal West Surrey
Regiment)
Born in Addlestone, 1896
Baptised, 1 November 1896, St Paul's, Addlestone
Son of George and Mary Deadman, née Knowles, of Row Hill,
Addlestone (1891 census) (m.1873)
Killed in action, 1 July 1916, France, on the first day of the Battle of the Somme, age 19
Memorial: THIEPVAL MEMORIAL, Somme, France

'By the letter of a comrade it is understood that Lc.-Cpl. Frank Deadman, of the Queen's R.W.S. Regt. – and the eldest son of Mr. S Deadman, of Rowhill – was killed in the British offensive on July 2nd. The letter, which reached the sisters of the young fellow (Mrs Cotton and Miss Deadman, of Alexandra-road), stated that he had been blown to pieces by the German artillery.

Lc.-Cpl. Deadman, who would not have reached his 20th birthday until next month, joined the Army nearly three years ago. For fully twelve months he had been in France, and about four months ago he was slightly gassed.' (The Surrey Herald, July 21, 1916)

DEAN, Ernest Hazell

Lance Corporal G/37069, 1st Bn. Queen's (Royal West Surrey
Regiment)
Born in Addlestone, 1898
Son of Ernest and Constance Laura Alice Dean, née Hazell, of The
White Hart, New Haw (m.1895)
Died of wounds, 26 October 1918, France, age 20
Cemetery: PREMONT BRITISH CEMETERY, Aisne, France

'Mr. and Mrs. Dean, of the White Hart Hotel, New Haw, have received information that their eldest son, Lce.-Corpl. Ernest H. Dean, was killed on the 26th of October. He joined the Army the week hostilities broke out, at the age of 16 years and four months, consequently he would have been 21 next March. Three times he

had been to France – once he was wounded and he had experienced trench fever. Prior to enlisting he worked for Messrs. Long and Long, electricians, Woking.' (The Surrey Herald, November 15, 1918)

DEDMAN, Frederick Newbart

Private 9828, 1st Bn. East Surrey Regiment
Enlisted, 10 February 1909
Born in New Haw, 1889
Baptised, 6 April 1890, St Paul's, Addlestone
Youngest son of William (d.1899) and Sarah Dedman, of Row Hill, Chertsey
Killed in action, 2 January 1915, near Wulverghem, Belgium, age 25
Memorial: YPRES (MENIN GATE) MEMORIAL, Ieper, West-Vlaanderen, Belgium

'Ottershaw has given of her sons freely in the greatest of all wars. The latest soldier from the little hamlet to die for his country is Lance-Corporal F. N. Dedman, of the 1st East surrey Regt. News has been received that Dedman was killed in action on January 2nd.

Lc.-Corpl. Dedman, whose widowed mother lives at Row Hill, was 25 years of age. Previously to joining the Regulars six years ago he was in the Chertsey Territorials for a couple of years, and in one shooting competition he secured the first prize. Before leaving for the Front he was Orderly at Kingston Barracks.' (The Surrey Herald, January 29, 1915)

'The mother of Lc.-Corpl. F. N. Dedman, 1st East Surrey Regiment (who was killed in action on January 2nd, as recorded in our last issue) has received the following interesting letter from the Lieutenant who was commanding his company.

"Dear Mrs Dedman, - Your letter of January 23rd to hand. I have given orders for the parcel you mention to be disposed of as you have directed. It was very nice of you to think of your poor son's comrades at such a time.

Allow me to offer you all my deepest sympathy in your great loss, which is also shared by me as your son was a very good N.C.O., and did excellent work during the time he was with the Battalion.

We were in the trenches when your son was unfortunately struck in the head by a bullet, death being practically instantaneous. He was given a battlefield burial and his grave is on the Wulverghem – Wychacte Road, about 600 yds out from Wulverghem (Belgium) and about –yds from the left hand side of the road." (The Surrey Herald, February 5, 1915)

DIVES, William

Private G/26186, 7th Bn. Buffs (East Kent Regiment)
Born in Walthamstow, 1891
Son of Daniel and the late Ellen Dives, of Mitcham, Surrey; husband of Maud Rosa Budd (formerly Dives, née Eales, m.1914) of "Sunnyside", New Haw Road, Addlestone
Died in hospital at Amiens, France, 21 October 1918, age 27
Cemetery: VILLERS-BRETONNEUX MILITARY CEMETERY, Somme, France

'PTE. W. DIVES, of The Buffs, succumbed to illness in a hospital at Amiens (France) on October 21st. His widow resides at Pagecroft, Chertsey-road.' (The Surrey Herald, November 1, 1918)

DOREY, Arthur Percy

Private 24015, 2nd Bn. Grenadier Guards
Born in Guildford, 1896
Son of David James and Eliza Ann Dorey, née Wetherall, of Century Rd., Staines, Middx. (m.1895)
Killed in action, 25 September 1916, France, during the Battle of Morval, part of the Battle of the Somme, age 19
Cemetery: GUARDS' CEMETERY, LESBOEUFS, Somme, France

'IN MEMORIAM
DOREY – In loving memory of our dear loved one, Arthur Percy Dorey, the eldest son of Mr. and Mrs. Dorey, killed in the Battle of Somme on 25th of Sept., 1916.

> *A bitter grief and shock severe,*
> *To part with one we loved so dear.*
> *It was God's wish, we'll not complain,*
> *But hope in heaven to meet again.*

From his sorrowing Mother and Father, Sister and Brothers.' (The Surrey Herald, September 28, 1917)

DREW, George Henry

Private 41660, 1st/5th Bn. South Staffordshire Regiment
Born in Camberwell, 1889; living in Alexandra Road, Addlestone (1911 census)
Son of George and Emily Drew, née Miller, of Camberwell, London (m.1888)
Died, 23 November 1918, Italy, age 29
Cemetery: MONTECCHIO PRECALCINO COMMUNAL CEMETERY EXTENSION, Italy

'PTE. G. DREW, now of the South Staffords, but who enlisted in Major Watney's A.S.C. column, is home on 14 day's leave from the Italian Front. Drew, well known for his football prowess, has been in France, Egypt, Salonica and Italy.' (The Surrey Herald, January 25, 1918)

DURRANT, William John

Private 19140, 8th Bn. East Surrey Regiment
Born in Richmond, Surrey 1897
Son of John Carmelite and Sarah Ann Durrant, née Curr, of Beaumont Avenue, Richmond (1911 census) (m.1895); grandson of William and Jane Durrant, of Spinney Hill, Addlestone (1911 census)
Killed in action, 3 May 1917, France, during the 3rd Battle of the Scarpe (part of the Arras Offensive), age 19
Memorial: ARRAS MEMORIAL, Pas de Calais, France

EAGLES, George Sawyer

Private G/24231, 1st Bn. Buffs (East Kent Regiment)
Born in Addlestone, 10 September 1898
Son of William Alfred G. and Harriett Jane Eagles, née Turner, of Wheatash Rd., Addlestone (m.1893)
Died, 1 December 1917, France, from wounds received on 20 November 1917, the first day of the Battle of Cambrai, age 19
Cemetery: ETAPLES MILITARY CEMETERY, Pas de Calais, France

'Mr. and Mrs. Eagles, of Wheatash-road, have received an official notification from the War Office, and also a letter from the sister-in-charge of a general hospital, France, stating that their son, Pte. George S. Eagles, of the Buffs, died of the wounds on the 1st December which he sustained on the 20th November.

The deceased soldier was 19 years of age. He enlisted in H.M. Forces in May of the present year, and had only seen about six weeks fighting on the Western Front. He was formerly employed at the Lang Propeller Works, and was an old boy of the St. James School, Weybridge.' (The Surrey Herald, December 14, 1917)

EDWARDS, Colin Hyde
See **HYDE-EDWARDS, Colin**

ELLIOTT, Bertie Victor
Private 68518, 7th Bn. Queen's (Royal West Surrey Regiment)
Born in Addlestone, 1899
Baptised, 10 September 1899, St Paul's, Addlestone
Youngest son of Samuel and Leah Elliott, née Francis, of Common Lane, New Haw (m.1883)
Killed in action, 24 October 1918, near the village of Robertsart, Belgium, about 20 km North West of Mons, during the final advance of the war, age 19
Cemetery: CROSS ROADS CEMETERY, FONTAINE-AU-BOIS, Nord, France

ELLIOTT, George Francis
Lance Corporal G/87799, 4th Bn. Duke of Cambridge's Own (Middlesex Regiment)
Born in Addlestone, 1889
Baptised, 29 December 1889, St Paul's, Addlestone
Son of Samuel and Leah Elliott, née Francis, of Common Lane, New Haw (m.1883)
Killed in action, 20 July 1918, near the village of Foncquevillers, France, about 17 km South West of Arras, age 28
Cemetery: ST. AMAND BRITISH CEMETERY, Pas de Calais, France

ELMS, William George

Private G/77846, 17th Bn. Royal Fusiliers (City of London Regiment)
Born in Addlestone, 1899
Baptised, 19 November 1899, St Paul's, Addlestone
Son of Harry George and Ellen Elms, née Hoare, of Chapel Park Road, Addlestone (m.1896)
Killed in action, 6 June 1918, France, age 18
Cemetery: BIENVILLERS MILITARY CEMETERY, Pas de Calais, France

'As briefly mentioned in our last issue, Pte. Wm. George Elms, of the Royal Fusiliers, son of Mr. H. Elms, of 7, Chapel Park, Addlestone, was killed in France on the night of June 6th by a shell. Mr. and Mrs. Elms, with whom much sympathy is evinced, have received a sympathetic letter from the deceased's Commanding Officer, who pays a high tribute to his excellence as a soldier. The Chaplain also writes, giving particulars of his burial and stating that he would be much missed.

The deceased was for many years in St. Paul's Church choir, and took the solo parts in some cantatas. He was a member of the Addlestone Cadet Corps connected with the Volunteers, to whom he was official bugler. Pte. Elms joined the Army as recently as Nov.

5th, and he had been in France three weeks when he was killed, at the age of 18 years 8 months. The deceased was very popular among a large circle of friends.

Pte. Elms, who was working for Mr P. Ricks when he joined the Colours, was home on leave 29 days before his death. For several years he was in the Chertsey Boys' Brigade, and at one meeting he secured the award for being the smartest boy in the Company. He played the "Last Post" at the funeral in Addlestone cemetery over the first local soldier (Pte. Sizmur) to be buried locally as the result of wounds.' (The Surrey Herald, June 28, 1918)

ETHERINGTON, William James

Private 10569, 1st Bn. East Surrey Regiment
Enlisted, 5 November 1912
Born in New Haw, 8 May 1895
Baptised, 30 March 1902, St Paul's, Addlestone
Son of Mrs Amy Marion Harman, née Etherington, of Beltran Road, Fulham
Killed in action, 23 August 1914, near the Mons-Condé canal, during the Battle of Mons, age 19
Cemetery: HAUTRAGE MILITARY CEMETERY, Saint-Ghislain, Hainaut, Belgium

FIELD, Alfred John Charles

Private 79221, 9th Bn. Royal Fusiliers (City of London Regiment)
Born in Albion Cottage, Liberty Hall Road, Addlestone, 25 May 1900
Baptised, 15 July 1900, St Paul's, Addlestone
Eldest son of Albert and Ellen Mary Field, née Bartram, of Victoria Road, Addlestone (1911 census) (m.1897)
Died of wounds, 27 August 1918, France, age 18
Cemetery: DAOURS COMMUNAL CEMETERY EXTENSION, Somme, France

'We regret to learn that Pte. A. J. Field, of the Royal Fusiliers, died from wounds on Aug. 27th. The deceased soldier enlisted as recently as last February, and went to France on Aug. 7th. He was 18¾ years of age. Before enlisting he was employed at Vickers Ltd., where he was in the machine shop for 10 months. Prior to that he was with the local Co-operative Society, and also worked as gardener to Mr. T. A. Rickman, J.P. He was the eldest son of Mr. A. Field, of 37, Liberty Hall-road.' (The Surrey Herald, September 20, 1918)

FIELD, George

Private 228084, 1st (City of London) Bn. (Royal Fusiliers) London Regiment
Born in Oatlands Park, Weybridge, 1882
Son of William and Mercy Field; husband of Ethel Emily Field, née Hall, of Marsh Lane, Addlestone (m.1907)
Killed in action, 26 April 1917, during the Arras Offensive, age 35
Memorial: ARRAS MEMORIAL, Pas de Calais, France

'With regret we have to record the death in France of yet another Addlestone soldier, in the person of Pte. George Field, of the Royal Fusiliers.

Mrs. Field, who resides in Simplemarsh-road, received the sad news of her husband's death on Tuesday morning by a letter from the Chaplain to the Forces. The following is an extract:- "By now no doubt you have heard that your husband was killed during operations in part of Arras between 22nd and 28th April. You will be comforted and proud to know that he fell with others while successfully driving back the enemy out here. We all feel so much for you at home in such times as these – you know so little, we know so much, and to us it is the loss of a friend, for you it is the loss of one very near and dear to you. We comfort ourselves chiefly to think that all this terrible sacrifice is a foundation upon which shall be built a far better state of things in the future. A cemetery was formed close to where your husband fell in which his body now rests."

The late Pte. Field was 35 years of age and prior to joining the Forces in December 1914, was an enthusiastic member of the Addlestone Company of the Surrey National Reserve. He enlisted in the Queen's R.W. Surrey Regt., but was later transferred to the Royal Fusiliers. He had crossed to France only one month before he met his death. The deceased, who leaves a widow and three children, was employed by the Coxe's Lock Milling Co. for 14 years before the outbreak of hostilities.' (The Surrey Herald, May 11, 1917)

FIELD, Thomas George

Private 2926, 7th Bn. Royal Welsh Fusiliers
Born in Spratts, Ottershaw, 1888
Son of George and Sarah Field, née Brown, of Liberty Hall Road,
Addlestone (1911 census) (m.1886)
Died of wounds at sea, 16 August 1915, after taking part in the
landings at Suvla Bay, Gallipoli Peninsula, on 9 August 1915, age 27
Memorial: HELLES MEMORIAL, Turkey

'Mr. and Mrs. George Field, of "Cambria", Spratts, Ottershaw, have received the sad news during the week to the effect that their eldest son, Thomas George Field, a private in the 1/7th Batt. of the Royal Welsh Fusiliers, died of wounds on the 16th of last month. Deceased, who was 27 years of age, joined the Army at the outbreak of war and sailed from this country in July last for an unknown destination. He wrote letters home from Devonport, Malta and Port Said and the last time his father and mother heard from him was while he was staying two or three days at the last named port. He has only been home once since enlisting, and that was in April last, for four days.

Mrs. Field seems to think that her son must have participated in the Gallipoli Peninsula operations and have taken part in the landing at Suvla Bay, which ranks as one of the most brilliant achievements in the annals of military history.

Pte. Field was born at Spratts and attended the Ottershaw School. Subsequently he started work as a gardener at Messrs. Fletchers' Nurseries, and after three years experience he went to Hatchford Park, Chobham, where he stayed 18 months, and following a similar period of work at Halstead in Essex, he went down to Hendrefoslan, near Swansea, for over two years, and for three years prior to the war he worked for Mr. J. Naylor, of Leighton Hall, Welsh Pool, North Wales. He was engaged to be married to Miss Priest, of Leighton Village.

The Field family are well-known and highly respected in the district, Mr. Field having for several years been the President of the Addlestone and District Co-operative Society, and he is now a member of the committee of management.

The deepest sympathy is expressed with Mr. and Mrs. Field and son in their sad bereavement.

The younger son, Mr Frank Field, joined the Royal Naval Air Service last November and he is stationed somewhere in Kent.

Mr. and Mrs. Field received a letter from Lord Kitchener conveying the true sympathy of the King and Queen in their sorrow.' (The Surrey Herald, September 17, 1915)

FREEMAN, Frederick Albert

Private 15551, 8th Bn. Princess Charlotte of Wales's (Royal Berkshire Regiment)
Born in Cippenham, Bucks., 1894
Son of Daniel and Rose Annie Freeman, née Snow, of Burnham, Bucks. (1901 census) (m.1882)
Killed in action, 25 September 1915, France, during the first day of the Battle of Loos, age 21
Cemetery: DUD CORNER CEMETERY, LOOS, Pas de Calais, France

'The death is announced of Pte. F. A. Freeman, a former member of the Addlestone Excelsior Band, who was killed in action on Sept. 25th. Deceased was a nephew of Mrs. J. Snow, of Hamm Moor, with whom he made his home. He enlisted in the Royal Berks. Regt. for the duration of the war, and was previously employed as a platelayer on the South Western Railway.' (The Surrey Herald, November 26, 1915)

FUIDGE, James Courtenay

Private 30135, 15th Bn. Royal Warwickshire Regiment
Formerly, Private 19701, Oxfordshire and Buckinghamshire Light Infantry
Born in Row Town, 8 June 1899
Baptised, 29 June 1899, St Paul's, Addlestone
Son of William Joseph and Florence Mary Fuidge, née Mead, of Liberty Hall Road, Addlestone (1911 census) (m.1896)
Killed in action, 24 September 1916, France, during the Battle of the Somme, age 17
Cemetery: GUARDS' CEMETERY, LESBOEUFS, Somme, France

'Yet another Addlestone soldier has made the supreme sacrifice for king and country. This time it is Lc.-Cpl. J. C. Fuidge, the second son of Mr. and Mrs. Fuidge, of Liberty Hall-road.

The deceased soldier, who was only 17 years of age, enlisted some 12 months ago, joining the Royal Warwickshire Regiment. He had been in France for only two months when he met his death.

The intimation was received by the parents on Wednesday morning, the 18th October, from the War Office. The official form stated that Lc.-Cpl. Fuidge was killed in action on the 24th Sept., during the heavy fighting on the Somme.

Prior to joining the Forces the young fellow was in the employ of Mr. Luxford, fruiterer, of Weybridge.' (The Surrey Herald, October 27, 1916)

GAY, James Henry

Shoeing Smith 43909, "A" Bty. 66th Bde. Royal Field Artillery
Born in Aldermaston, 1877
Son of John and Mary Gay, of Aldermaston, Berks; husband of Martha Mary Gay, née Luckhurst, of Chestnut Grove, Staines, Middx. (m.1908)
Died, 25 February 1917, Mesopotamia, age 40
Cemetery: AMARA WAR CEMETERY, Iraq

'News has been received of the death, in hospital in Mesopotamia, of Shoeing-Smith J. H. Gay, of the Royal Field Artillery, on February 25th.

Although a resident of Addlestone only a short time, deceased was respected by many. Previously to the war he was in the employ of Mr. W. Woodger and Messrs. F. Hayes and Son, both of Addlestone. S.S. Gay leaves a widow to mourn her loss, her home being at 34, Ecton-road.

Mrs. Gay wishes to thank all the kind friends who have expressed sympathy with her in her sorrow.' (The Surrey Herald, March 23, 1917)

GOSDEN, George Herbert

Rifleman R/10441, 8th Bn. King's Royal Rifle Corps
Born in Addlestone, 1896
Baptised, 2 February 1896, St Paul's, Addlestone
Son of Henry and Annie Gosden, née Hurley, of Chapel Avenue,
Addlestone (m.1888)
Killed in action, 1 July 1916, near Arras, France, age 20
Cemetery: TILLOY BRITISH CEMETERY, TILLOY-LES-
MOFFLAINES,
Pas de Calais, France

'We regret having to announce the death of yet another Addlestone soldier – Pte. G. H. Gosden, the youngest son of Mr. and Mrs. H. Gosden, of 27, Chapel Avenue.

Pte. Gosden enlisted in March, 1915, joining the King's Royal Rifles. After undergoing the brief training of three months he was sent over to France. In August – a couple of months later – he was wounded by a bullet in the thigh, which necessitated him spending two months in an English hospital. However, he returned to France only to be again incapacitated in December by frost-bitten feet. Only three weeks before his death he was again wounded by shrapnel in the right hand.

The parents received an official intimation from the War Office on July 30th, stating that Pte. Gosden had been reported missing after an engagement on July 2nd. A letter from the captain of the Regiment was received on the 14th August, which contradicted the War Office statement. The officer wrote: "Your son was killed in action on the 1st July, and I am very glad to say he suffered no pain. He was buried at Arras and a wooden cross bearing his name and regiment was erected over his grave. The lad was loved by all his comrades. We looked upon him as a brave man and his loss is felt by all."

The deceased soldier was well-known in the Addlestone district. He was a member of the Addlestone Band for 11 years. Pte. Gosden was only 20 years of age, and prior to enlisting he was employed as a gardener by Mr. Pettitt, of Walton. Mr. and Mrs. Gosden have two other sons serving – one in the Royal Inniskilling Fusiliers (also in France), and the other in the Navy, as a stoker on one of H.M. ships of war.' (The Surrey Herald, August 25, 1916)

GRANT, Frank

Motor Mechanic MB/2627, Royal Naval Volunteer Reserve; Motor Boat
Reserve H.M.M. L "403" R.N. Div.
Born in Addlestone, 1898
Son of William and Sarah Alice Grant, née Lashwood, of Ongar Road,
Addlestone (m.1879)
Killed, 22 August 1918, age 19
Cemetery: HINDERWELL CEMETERY, Yorkshire, United Kingdom

    *'The sympathy of our readers will be extended to Mr. and Mrs. A.
Grant, of 23, Ongar-road, who during the weekend learned that their
son, Second Eng. Frank Grant, had met his death whilst helping to salve an enemy
torpedo. The deceased, who was only 19 years of age, was on one of H.M. motor launches
engaged in patrol work.*

    *Lieut. A. Ross, R.N.V.R., has written to the parents: "Your son had been on the ship
only a few weeks, but in that short time I found him a most promising lad, and deplore his
untimely end. He was a most reliable, conscientious and capable lad, and is a great loss
to the Service.*

    *I am aware that nothing can console you for the loss of your son, but it may be a little
satisfaction to you to know that he was appreciated as a good lad and a member of the
Service by all of us. The officers and men on the base join me in expressing deepest
sympathy with you in your grievous loss." (The Surrey Herald, September 6, 1918)*

GREEN, Arthur Page

Private G/39861, 1st Bn. Queen's (Royal West Surrey Regiment)
Born in Addlestone, 1883
Baptised, 27 November 1890, St Paul's, Addlestone
Son of Henry and Julia Elizabeth Green, née Page, of Addlestone Hill; husband of
Elizabeth Green, née Worts, of Queen's Road, Teddington (m.1909)
Killed in action, 25 September 1917, near Gheluvelt, Belgium, during the Third Battle of
Ypres (Passchendaele), age 34
Cemetery: TYNE COT CEMETERY, Zonnebeke, West-Vlaanderen, Belgium

    *'Mr. and Mrs. H. Green, of Addlestone Hill, have learned by an official notification that
their second son, Pte. Arthur P. Green, of the Machine Gun Section, Queen's R.W. Surrey
Regt., has been posted as missing after the fighting on the 25th Sept. Pte. Green crossed
to France early in August of the present year. He is 34 years of age, and married, his wife
residing at Teddington.*

    *It is only about three months ago that the parents' third son, Lc-Cpl. Claude Green, of
the Sussex Regt., was killed in action. The youngest son is at present serving in France
with the R.A.M.C.' (The Surrey Herald, November 9, 1917)*

GREEN, Claud

Lance Corporal G/17984, "C" Coy. 13th Bn. Royal Sussex Regiment
Born in Addlestone, 1889
Baptised, 27 November 1890, St Paul's, Addlestone
Son of Henry and Julia Elizabeth Green, née Page, of Addlestone Hill (m.1875)
Killed in action, 31 July 1917, Belgium, during the Battle of Pilckem, Third Battle of Ypres (Passchendaele), age 28
Memorial: YPRES (MENIN GATE) MEMORIAL, Ieper, West-Vlaanderen, Belgium

'On Friday morning the news reached Mr. and Mrs. Green, of Addlestone Hill, that their son, Lc.-Cpl. Claude Green, of the Royal Sussex Regt., had made the great sacrifice in France on July 31st.

Born in Addlestone 28 years ago, Lc. Cpl. Green on leaving school passed into the employment of Mr. A. Hobson, grocer, following one brother in the same shop and, years afterwards, having another brother follow him, so that three brothers have been in the same employ. Claud Green passed into the employment of Messrs. Tyler, of Guildford, and was one of their leading hands when he joined H.M. Forces. The deceased N.C.O., who was single, was of a merry disposition, and he had a host of friends. He crossed to France about 12 months ago.

The intimation reached the parents through the subjoined letter from Capt. Clarence G. Walker, the officer commanding deceased's company:-

"It is with great regret that I have to inform you of the death in action of your son, Lance-Cpl. Green, of the company under my command, on 31st July last. He was gallantly leading his section in the recent attack, and was instantaneously killed by a sniper's bullet. His loss is keenly felt by all his comrades and all who knew him. Please accept the heartfelt condolences of us all in your sad bereavement."

Mr. and Mrs. Green have two other sons serving in France, and a third has been invalided from the Navy.' (The Surrey Herald, August 17, 1917)

GREGORY, Albert James

Rifleman 3871, 1/9th (County of London) Bn. London Regiment (Queen Victoria's Rifles)
Born in Byfleet, 3 May 1898
Baptised, 3 July 1898, St Mary's, Byfleet
Third son of George Frederick and Elizabeth Fanny Gregory, née Dunce, of Rose Gardens, Woodham Lane, New Haw, Addlestone (m.1890)
Killed in action, 1 July 1916, France, on the first day of the Battle of the Somme, during the attack towards Gommecourt, age 18
Memorial: THIEPVAL MEMORIAL, Somme, France

'The mother of Rifleman Albert J. Gregory, of the Queen Victoria Rifles, who resides at 4 Rose Gardens, Woodham-road, Addlestone, has been officially informed by the War Office that he has been killed. The deceased was reported to be missing after July 1st of last year, on which day he took part in an attack on the German trenches. His parents have since made every effort to ascertain if he had survived, but unsuccessfully. The deceased joined up at the age of 16½ years. He had been a Scout, and was employed in London before the war.

The deceased's parents came to live at Addlestone about six years ago. Before that they resided at Byfleet, where young Gregory was in St. Mary's Church choir.' (The Surrey Herald, April 27, 1917)

GROOM, Archie Vernon

Rifleman 6443, 1/8th (City of London) Bn. London Regiment (Post Office Rifles)
Born in Addlestone, 1893
Son of Frank and Annie Groom, née Punter, of Paris Barne Cottage, West Byfleet (m.1891)
Killed in action, 7 October 1916, France, while taking part in an attack on the village of Le Sars, during the Battle of the Somme, age 23
Memorial: THIEPVAL MEMORIAL, Somme, France

'So far all efforts to trace Rifleman A. V. Groom, of Newhaw, have been unsuccessful. As recorded in our columns shortly afterwards, the young fellow was reported wounded and missing after the fighting on Oct. 7th, and another official communication just received merely confirms that, without furnishing any details. His uncle and aunt, Mr. and Mrs. H. Groom, of Rose Cottage, Newhaw-road, will appreciate any information from those serving in his Battalion of the London Regt. at the Front.' (The Surrey Herald, December 8, 1916)

GROOM, Arthur Henry

Bombardier 27309, 10th Siege Bty. Royal Garrison Artillery
Born in Addlestone, 1886
Son of Charles and Sarah Groom, of Victoria Road, Addlestone (1911 census); husband of Elizabeth J. Groom, née Joiner, of Brighton (m.1916)
Killed in action, 29 February 1916, France & Flanders, age 30
Cemetery: DICKEBUSCH NEW MILITARY CEMETERY, Ieper, West-Vlaanderen, Belgium

'The sad news reached Mr. and Mrs. Groom, of Albert-road, on Sunday morning that their son, Bombardier Arthur (Arch.) Groom, had been killed in action, in France, on Feb. 29th.

The deceased Bombardier had nine years service to his credit, and he had seen fully twelve month's strenuous fighting in France. Previously to joining the Colours he was well known as a member of local football teams, also as a runner with the Weybridge Harriers. His keenness in sport was continued when he joined the Royal Garrison Artillery, for he represented his Battery in many football tournaments at home and abroad.

Whilst at home on a few days leave in January, Bombardier Groom was married to a young lady staying in Addlestone, but who is now living at Brighton. His brother, Vernon, of the Royal Horse Artillery, was wounded in the retreat from Mons, and was one of the first local soldiers to reach home from the Front.

Mr. and Mrs. Groom and family wish to thank all those who have sympathised with them in their loss.' (The Surrey Herald, March 17, 1916)

GURNEY, Thomas George

Private 353426, 1/7th (City of London) Bn. London Regiment
Born in Addlestone, 1896
Son of William and Emily Kate Gurney, née Tarr, of Common Lane,
New Haw, Addlestone (m.1886)
Killed in action, 7 October 1916, France, while taking part in an
attack on the Butte de Warlencourt, during the Battle of the Somme,
age 20
Memorial: THIEPVAL MEMORIAL, Somme, France
(Photograph: courtesy of Mr R Gurney)

'We recorded in our last issue the experiences of a Weybridge
soldier in a shell crater, where for six days and nights he remained without food. It was
mentioned that he was with two other companions (one being an Addlestone soldier), who
both died. We now learn that the Addlestone soldier was Pte. George Gurney, of
Common-lane, New Haw.

The deceased soldier, who enlisted on the outbreak of war in the East Surrey Regt., was
later transferred to the City of Londons. He had been in France only five weeks when he
met his death from wounds and hardship in the shell crater. The parents were recently
notified by the War Office that their son had been returned as missing, but the
information from Pte. England shows that their son died in the crater. The deceased was
20 years of age and prior to joining the Forces was employed by the Anglo-American Oil
Co.' (The Surrey Herald, November 17, 1916)

HADDEN, Archibald Robert

Captain, 1/9th (County of London) Bn. London Regiment (Queen Victoria's Rifles)
Commissioned as Second Lieutenant, 4 February 1909, Territorial Force. Applied to join
Expeditionary Force in December 1916
Born in Tower Hamlets, London, 28 November 1889
Elder son of the late Rev. Robert Henry and Eva Prudence Hadden, née Evans, of Hazel
Hatch, Ongar Hill, Addlestone; husband of Evelyn Forster Hadden, née Tunnicliffe, of
The Lees, Great Malvern, Worcs. (m.1915)
Killed in action, 25 April 1918, near the village of Hangard, Somme, France, during the
German spring offensive, age 29
Cemetery: HANGARD COMMUNAL CEMETERY EXTENSION, Somme, France

'Previously reported missing, now officially assumed killed in action on April 25th,
1918, at Hangard Wood, Captain Archibald Robert Hadden, 9th London Regt. (Queen
Victoria's Rifles), elder and only surviving son of the late Rev. R.H. Hadden, M.A., Vicar
of St. Mark's, North Audley-street, W., Chaplain in ordinary to H.M. Queen Victoria and
Hon. Chaplain to H.M. King Edward VII, and of Mrs Hadden of Hazel Hatch,
Addlestone, Surrey, and husband of Evelyn Forster Hadden, also of Hazel Hatch.' (The
Surrey Herald, March 21, 1919)

HADDEN, Eustace Walter Russell

Major, 1/4th Bn. Oxfordshire and Buckinghamshire Light Infantry
Born in Holborn, London, 1891
Younger son of the late Rev. Robert Henry and Eva Prudence Hadden, née Evans, of
Hazel Hatch, Ongar Hill, Addlestone (m.1888)
Died, 11 June 1916, France, age 25
Cemetery: ABBEVILLE COMMUNAL CEMETERY, Somme, France

HAINES, George Henry

Stoker 2nd Class, K/35519, H.M.S. *Vanguard*, Royal Navy
Born in Nether Compton, Dorset, 31 March 1885
Younger son of George and Ann Haines, née Garrett, of Australian Cottages, Woodham Lane, New Haw, Addlestone; husband of Daisy Haines, née Bond, of Fairfield Terrace, Staines (m.1915); uncle of Leonard Percy Frank A'Court, also a fatal casualty
Killed, 9 July 1917, 11.20pm, Scapa Flow, when H.M.S. Vanguard, a Dreadnought battleship of 19,250 tons, exploded and sank while at anchor. 804 officers and men were lost, two survived. Age 32
Memorial: CHATHAM NAVAL MEMORIAL, Kent, United Kingdom

'Among the victims of the Vanguard disaster, which occurred on the 9th inst, must be included a New Haw sailor in the person of 2nd Class Stoker George Henry Haine, whose wife resides at No. 5, Davis Cottages, Woodham Lane. The official notification from the Admiralty reached Mrs. Haine last Friday morning.

The deceased stoker was 31 years of age. He had served 13 years in the Army, including six in India. On the outbreak of war he was called up with the Reserve, and he crossed to France with the original Expeditionary Force, being attached to the Royal Dragoon Guards. He was, however, in France only about three months when he was injured by a horse. He returned to England, and was granted his discharge in October, 1915. About 12 months ago he was called up for re-examination, and on being passed he entered the Navy. He had been on the Vanguard only since last January.

The deceased leaves a widow and two children. Mrs Haine was expecting her husband home on leave within a few weeks.' (The Surrey Herald, July 20, 1917)

HALEY, Albert Lancelot

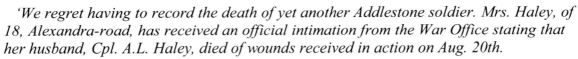

Corporal G/12697, 4th Bn. Royal Fusiliers (City of London Regiment)
Born in Teddington, 1882
Son of James and Emma Haley, of Teddington, Middx.; husband of Annie Haley, née Gwilliam, of Alexandra Road, Addlestone (m.1903)
Died of wounds, 20 August 1916, France, sustained during the Battle of the Somme, age 34
Cemetery: LA NEUVILLE BRITISH CEMETERY, CORBIE, Somme, France

'We regret having to record the death of yet another Addlestone soldier. Mrs. Haley, of 18, Alexandra-road, has received an official intimation from the War Office stating that her husband, Cpl. A.L. Haley, died of wounds received in action on Aug. 20th.

Cpl. Haley joined the Forces in February, 1915, passing into the 4th Battn. of the Royal Fusiliers. He sailed for France the following January. The deceased soldier was well-known to passengers at Addlestone Station, where he worked as a porter for six years. He had been employed by the L. and S.W. Railway Co. as a porter for 11 years.

Cpl. Haley was 35 years of age, and he leaves a wife and three children to mourn their loss. Mrs. Haley is at present acting as a 'postwoman' at the Weybridge Post Office.' (The Surrey Herald, September 15, 1916)

HALL, Frederick Francis
Rifleman 206263, 24th Bn. Rifle Brigade (The Prince Consort's Own)
Born in Addlestone, 1873
Son of Francis Hall, of Addlestone; husband of Florence Susan Hall, née Watts, of Chapel Grove, Addlestone (m.1902)
Died of pneumonia, 22 May 1919, near Port Said, Egypt, age 45
Also served in India and in the South African War
Cemetery: PORT SAID WAR MEMORIAL CEMETERY, Egypt

HAMPTON, Arthur Lawrence
Private 34282, 1/6th Bn. East Surrey Regiment
Born Weybridge, 4 March 1893
Son of Henry George and Flora Hampton, née Pizzey, of Rose Mount, Liberty Lane, Addlestone (1911 census); husband of Winifred Hampton, née Theobald, of Station Road, Addlestone (m.1917)
Died, 28 October 1918, Jullunder, India, age 25
Memorial: MADRAS 1914-1918 WAR MEMORIAL, CHENNAI, India

'A young soldier well-known in Addlestone has succumbed to influenza in India, is Pte. Arthur Lawrence Hampton, whose widow lives at 97, Station-road, and whose parents were Mr. and Mrs. Hampton, senr., of Newhaw. The notification reached Mrs. Hampton, junr. on Friday last. The deceased, who had been stationed with the East Surreys at Agra, had died at Jullunder.

Pte. A. L. Hampton joined the Army 18 months ago, after three rejections, and he went to India about 12 months since. When he enlisted he was with Mr. Adams, hairdresser, Weybridge, but for eight years previously he had been with Mr. S. Clarke, Addlestone, consequently he was exceedingly well known in the locality.' (The Surrey Herald, November 15, 1918)

HAWKINS, Arthur Charles
Airman 2nd Class 1307, 4th Sqdn., Royal Flying Corps
Born in Surbiton, 1894
Son of Charles and Alice Mary Hawkins, née Werrell, of Station Road, Addlestone (m.1892)
Died, 5 February 1915, France, age 21
Cemetery: LONGUENESSE (ST. OMER) SOUVENIR CEMETERY, Pas de Calais, France

HEAD, Edwin Thomas Charles
Rifleman 318108, 1/5th (City of London) Bn. London Regiment (London Rifle Brigade)
Formerly 7230, 15th London Regiment
Born in Chertsey, 1898
Son of Thomas Edwin and Caroline Ethel Head, née West, of Pear Tree Road, Addlestone (m.1894)
Killed in action, 23 March 1918, France, age 20
Cemetery: ROCLINCOURT MILITARY CEMETERY, Pas de Calais, France

HIGGS, William Evans
Private 16451, 3rd Bn. Royal Fusiliers (City of London Regiment)
Born about 1890
Foster son of William Aaron and Sarah Ellen Bragg, née Clarke, of Chapel Park Road, Addlestone
Killed in action, 24 May 1915, Belgium, during the Second Battle of Ypres, age 25
Memorial: YPRES (MENIN GATE) MEMORIAL, Ieper, West-Vlaanderen, Belgium

'Mrs. Bragg, of 3, Chapel Park Road, adopted Higgs as her son. He belonged to the Royal Fusiliers (City of London Regiment) and joined the Forces in November last, being previously a porter at a grocery store at Weybridge. Leaving for France on May 17th, it was only seven days afterwards that he was reported missing. It has been rumoured in the village that he was killed, but this lacks confirmation.
Higgs, who was twenty-four years of age, was for some years with Mr. Lilley, of Chertsey, where he learned the hairdressing.' (The Surrey Herald, July 9, 1915)

HIGHAM, Eric Edward (born HYAM)
Lieutenant, 5th (City of London) Bn. London Regiment (London Rifle Brigade)
Born in Kensington, London, 1 September 1891
Son of David Edward and Emmie Higham, née Isaac, of "Coombelands", Addlestone (1901 census) (m.1890)
Died, 28 November 1922, Wimpole Street, London W1, from a head wound received on 9 September 1917, France, age 31

'Mr. and Mrs. D. E. Higham, of Coombelands, have received information to the effect that their son, Sec.-Lieut. E. E. Higham, of the London Rifle Brigade, is lying in hospital, having been seriously wounded in France.' (The Surrey Herald, September 21, 1917)

HILEY, Charles
Details unknown

HOADE, Reginald William

Second Lieutenant, 2/7th Bn. Duke of Cambridge's Own (Middlesex Regiment), attached to 1st Bn.
Born in Addlestone, 13 March 1890
Baptised, 15 May 1890, St Paul's, Addlestone
Elder son of William and Elizabeth Hoade, née Adams, of Oakley Lodge, Addlestone (1911 census) (m.1888); brother of Second Lieutenant John Robert Hoade
Killed in action, 15 July 1916, near High Wood, during the Battle of the Somme, age 26
Memorial: THIEPVAL MEMORIAL, Somme, France
Memorial window: St. Paul's, Addlestone, destroyed by fire in 2003 and not included in the restoration

'An official intimation reached Mr. and Mrs. Hoade, Oakley Lodge, on Saturday, that their elder son, Sec.-Lieut. R. W. Hoade, Middlesex Regt., had been killed in the course of the British offensive movement.
Readers will recollect that in our issue of July 21st it was recorded that the two sons of Mr. and Mrs. Hoade had both been wounded. It was known that the younger son, Sec.-Lieut. J. R. Hoade, had received four shrapnel wounds in the right arm, but no tidings

had been received concerning their elder son. As mentioned in our last issue, the parents subsequently received official information that Sec.-Lieut. R. W. Hoade had been killed, and this was verified by Saturday's communication.

The deceased officer, now known to have been killed in action on July 15th, was 26 years of age. He was educated at St. George's College, Weybridge, and will be remembered by many old Georgeians for his interest in sport, particularly cricket. He was made an underwriting member of Lloyds in 1911. When war broke out he joined, in company with his brother, the Inns of Court O.T.C., and in July, 1915, was awarded his commission in the Middlesex Regt. A month later he went to Gibraltar, and five months afterwards to Egypt, where he took part in the desert campaign against the Senussi. In May of the present year the brothers journeyed to France, in preparation for the British offensive.' (The Surrey Herald, August 11, 1916)

HOARE, John

Corporal S/4370, 13th Bn. Rifle Brigade (The Prince Consort's Own)
Born in Worplesdon, 1887
Elder son of John and Mary Ann Hoare, née Woods, of New Haw Road, New Haw (Register of Electors 1922) (m.1885); husband of Mary Elizabeth Hoare, née Nally, of Carlisle Street, St Marylebone, London (m.1909); father of three children
Killed in action, 7 August 1916, France, near Mametz Wood, during the Battle of the Somme, when his battalion suffered heavy shell-fire while in the line. Age 29
Cemetery: FLATIRON COPSE CEMETERY, MAMETZ, Somme, France

HORNE, Percival George

Private G/13894, 10th Bn, Queen's (Royal West Surrey Regiment)
Born in Folkestone, 1880
Son of George and Jane Horne; husband of Eleanor Annette Horne, née Montgomery, of Chapel Grove, Addlestone (1911 census) (m.1904)
Killed in action, 24 February 1917, Belgium, during an attack on the Hollandscheschuur Salient, near Ypres, age 36
Cemetery: KLEIN-VIERSTRAAT BRITISH CEMETERY, Heuvelland, West-Vlaanderen, Belgium

'HORNE – In proud and loving memory of our dear father, Pte. P. G. Horne, killed in France, Feb. 24th, 1917: also in ever loving memory of our dear mother, Nettie Horne, who died March 29th, 1918.
Keep our loved ones, Heavenly Father, beneath Thy care.
Percy, Ronnie and Arthur.' (The Surrey Herald, February 22, 1918)

HORROD, George

Private G/15548, 6th Bn. Queen's (Royal West Surrey Regiment)
Born in Harrow Weald, Middlesex, 1886
Son of George and Harriett Horrod, of Houblon Road, Richmond; husband of Madeline Horrod, née Hunt, of Peartree Road, Addlestone (m.1913)
Killed in action, 27 September 1918, near the St Quentin Canal, France, during the final British offensive of the war, age 32
Memorial: VIS-EN-ARTOIS MEMORIAL, Pas de Calais, France

HUNER, John Baden

Rifleman 575161, 17th (County of London) Bn. London Regiment (Poplar and Stepney Rifles)
Born in Addlestone, 1900
Son of John (d.1920) and Alice Huner, née Woodman (d.1908), of Ecton Road, Addlestone (1901 census) (m.1890)
Died, 4 September 1919, in Purfleet Military Hospital, age 18
Cemetery: ADDLESTONE BURIAL GROUND, Surrey, United Kingdom

'Much sympathy has been expressed with Mr. and Mrs. J. Huner, of 21, Ecton-road, in the bereavement they have sustained by the death of their son, Pte. John Baden Huner, of the 17th London Regt., who passed away very suddenly during Thursday last from septic poisoning.

The deceased – who would have attained the age of 19 next month – joined the Forces in October of last year. During the past few months he had been stationed at Purfleet. On Tuesday the 2nd Sept. he went into hospital, when two operations were found to be necessary, but despite the skill and care of the hospital staff death took place two days later.

The young soldier was well-known in the village, being a native of the place. He was well-liked and had a bright disposition.

The body was interred with military honours on Tuesday afternoon, in the Addlestone cemetery. A service was held at the Baptist Church, being conducted by the Rev. Sheers, of Weybridge. The coffin was covered with the Union Jack. Three volleys were fired over the graveside, and the Last Post was sounded.

The immediate mourners were: Father and Mother and Roland; Mrs. Hill and Mrs. Hames (sister); Sert.-Maj. and Mrs. Ede (brother-in-law and sister); Mrs. Mann and Mrs Ruffle (aunts); Mr. and Mrs. H. Woodman (aunt and uncle); Mrs A. Woodman (aunt); Mrs Pidwell (aunt). There were large numbers of friends both at the church and graveside.

Numbers of beautiful floral tributes were placed on the grave, including two from the deceased's Regiment and one from the teachers and children of the Baptist Sunday School.' (The Surrey Herald, September 12, 1919)

HYDE-EDWARDS, Colin

Second Lieutenant, 1st Bn. East Surrey Regiment
Born in Addlestone, 25 January 1897
Baptised, 20 March 1897, St Paul's, Addlestone
Youngest son of Lt. Col. Frederick William and Julia Annie Hyde-Edwards, née Humphery, of "Penton", Crouch Oak Lane, Addlestone (m.1888)
Education: Bradfield College, Berkshire
Died from gunshot wound, 22 May 1917, while a prisoner of war in the Field Hospital, St Clotilde, Douai, age 20
Cemetery: DOUAI COMMUNAL CEMETERY, Nord, France

'The sympathy of our readers will be extended to Lieut.-Col. and Mrs. Hyde Edwards in the loss they have sustained by the death of their youngest son, Sec.-Lieut. Colin Hyde Edwards, of the East Surrey Regt. Late in May of the present year Sec.-Lieut. Hyde Edwards was reported as missing from May 8th, but it has recently been established that he died of wounds as a prisoner of war on May 22nd. He was only 20 years of age, and had proved himself an enthusiastic young officer of the Regiment with which his father was for so long associated.' (The Surrey Herald, September 28, 1917)

JOYCE, Arthur
Private 20002, 10th Bn. Hampshire Regiment
Born in Addlestone, 1896
Baptised, 21 June 1896, St Paul's, Addlestone
Son of George Thomas and Martha Ann Joyce, née Payne, of Station Road, Addlestone (1911 census) (m.1881)
Killed in action, 1 September 1918, Macedonia, during the capture of the Roche Noire Salient, age 22
Cemetery: KARASOULI MILITARY CEMETERY, Greece

JOYCE, Herbert George
Private G/18443, 1st Bn. Queen's (Royal West Surrey Regiment)
Born in Barnes, 1882
Oldest son of George Thomas and Martha Ann Joyce, née Payne, of Station Road, Addlestone (1911 census); husband of Alice Daisy Joyce, née Mildenhall, (b. Kenley, nr. Croydon) (m.1911)
Killed in action, 25 September 1917, Belgium, near Gheluvelt, during the Third Battle of Ypres (Passchendaele), age 35
Memorial: TYNE COT MEMORIAL, Zonnebeke, West-Vlaanderen, Belgium

KEMP, Harry William
Private 18415, 3rd Bn. Coldstream Guards
Born in Paglesham, Essex, 1885
Son of Alfred and Emily Kemp, of Paglesham, Rochford, Essex; husband of Edith Elizabeth Dow, formerly Kemp, née Woolf, of The Harbour, Stambridge Road, Rochford, Essex (m.1911)
Killed in action, 13 April 1918, France, in the defence of Hazebrouck by the 4th Guards Brigade during the Battles of the Lys - part of the German Spring offensive, age 32
Memorial: PLOEGSTEERT MEMORIAL, Comines-Warneton, Hainaut, Belgium

'Previously reported missing since the great fight of the Guards on April 13th, Mrs Kemp, of The Cedars Cottage, has now been officially notified that her husband – Pte. Harry Kemp, the Coldstream Guards – must have been killed on that date. The deceased had for several years been head gardener to Mr. Geo. Edwards. He enlisted in May, 1916, and had been in France for 15 months, with one home leave last January. Mrs Kemp has one little boy of five.' (The Surrey Herald, July 26, 1918)

KINGTON, Edwin
Lieutenant, 11th Bde. Royal Field Artillery
Enlisted, as Gunner in RFA, 11 July 1899; commissioned, 2nd Lt., 17 December 1914
Born in Sunninghill, Berkshire, 1883
Son of William Edwin and Frances A. Kington, of "Newlands", Spinney Hill, Addlestone (Kelly's Directory 1918); husband of Maud Kington, née Symonds, of Elphinstone Road, Poona, India (m. 5 April 1911, Bangalore, India)
Died of wounds, 17 September 1916, received in action during the Battle of the Somme, age 33
Cemetery: PUCHEVILLERS BRITISH CEMETERY, Somme, France

'In the list of those mentioned in Sir John French's dispatches for "gallant and distinguished service in the field" occurs the name of 2nd Lieutenant E. Kington, Royal Field Artillery, a son of Mr. and Mrs. W. Kington, of Newlands, Spinney Hill, Addlestone.

*His friends congratulate him on the honour, and wish him every success in his career.'
(The Surrey Herald, June 25, 1915)*

LANGFIELD, Frank

Private G/45908, Queen's (Royal West Surrey Regiment); transferred to 425th
Agricultural Coy.
Born in Bagshot, 5 December 1892
Son of Emily Langfield, née Ridger, (m.William Henry Langfield 1881); husband of Rose
M. Langfield, née Dedman, of Rose Cottage, Row Hill, Addlestone (m.1914)
Died, 24 February 1919, age 26
Cemetery: ADDLESTONE BURIAL GROUND, Surrey, United Kingdom

LEWINGTON, William Eli

Private S/750, 2nd Bn. Queen's (Royal West Surrey Regiment)
Born in Chertsey, 1883
Son of Charles (d.1908) and Jemima Lewington, née Baigent, of
Spratts, Ottershaw (m.1877)
Killed in action, 16 May 1915, France, while attacking German lines
during the Battle of Festubert (Second Battle of Ypres), age 31
Memorial: LE TOURET MEMORIAL, Pas de Calais, France

*'Mrs. Lewington, of Spratts, Ottershaw, received the sad news on Wednesday, through
an official intimation from the War Office, that her third son, Pte. E. Lewington, the
Queen's (West Surrey Regiment), had been killed in action in France on May 16th.*

*Pte. Lewington served in the East Surrey Regiment for twelve years, half of the time
being spent in India. When war broke out he rejoined the Forces, but transferred his
attention to the Queen's.*

*Mrs. Lewington has another son in the Mechanical Transport section of the Army
Service Corps, he having joined up in the section raised at Weybridge by Major Gordon
Watney.' (The Surrey Herald, June 18, 1915)*

LIGHT, Frank

Sergeant S/756, 7th Bn. Queen's (Royal West Surrey Regiment)
Private 895, 3rd Bn. Queen's (Royal West Surrey Regiment) (South
African War 1899-1902)
Born in The Common, Weybridge, 8 May 1883
Baptised, 3 June 1883, St James', Weybridge
Third son of John and Mary Light, née Kersley, of Weybridge; husband
of Emma Light, née Dorsett, of Bourne Villa, New Haw Road, New
Haw, Addlestone (Register of Electors 1918) (m. 14 September 1902)
Killed in action, 1 July 1916, France, on the first day of the Battle of the Somme, during
the attack towards Montauban, age 33
Memorial: THIEPVAL MEMORIAL, Somme, France

*'The friends of Sergt. F. Light, of The Queen's Regt., whose wife and family reside at
Bourne Villa, New Haw Road, will be sorry to hear of his death. Sergt. Light, who
answered Lord Kitchener's appeal for instructors in September, 1914, had been for
twelve months in the trenches. He was in the employ of the Coxe's Lock Milling Co., Ltd.,
and was a member of the Co-operative Society. He also served as a member of the
committee of the Surrey National Reserve from its birth.*

Sergt. Light served in South Africa during the Boer War for two years and three months with the Queen's Regt.

The deceased, who was 33 years of age, was a bombing sergeant, and he was killed whilst leading his men from the trenches in a bombing attack. He leaves a widow and six children, one of whom has been a cripple during the past five years.

Two brothers have also seen considerable service. Sergt. H. G. Light, The Queen's Regt., has been missing since Loos, but was recently reported as wounded and a prisoner of war. Sergt. G. Light, of the Middlesex Regt., was wounded at Mons, and went out to France again, but after a few months had his feet frost-bitten, and is now in England. Regimental Q.M.S. Fred Light is serving with the Queen's Regt. at Shoreham.

The deceased had been very warmly recommended by his superiors, and it was anticipated that he would shortly have been granted a commission.' (The Surrey Herald, July 21, 1916)

LITTLEPROUD, William Frank
Private G/13446, 11th Bn. Queen's (Royal West Surrey Regiment)
Born in Hampton Wick, Kingston, 4 February 1886
Son of William George and Hannah Maria Littleproud, née Cox, of Hampton Wick; husband of Alice Littleproud, née Edwin, of High Street, Gosport, Hants., (m.10 May 1905); previously, Kings Road, New Haw, Addlestone (Register of Electors 1918)
Died of wounds, 7 October 1916, France, during the Battle of the Somme. The battalion had been in action near Flers and Mametz Wood during the previous weeks, age 30
Cemetery: ETAPLES MILITARY CEMETERY, Pas de Calais, France

MACE, George William
Private 32390, 63rd Provisional Coy. Royal Defence Corps
Formerly 20144, Queen's (Royal West Surrey Regiment)
Born in Deal, Kent, 1859
Baptised, 29 May 1859, St George's, Deal
Son of George and Mary Anne Mace of Deal: husband of Emily Mary Mace, née Tagg, of Liberty Hall Road, Addlestone (m.1882)
Died, 4 December 1916, United Kingdom, age 57
Cemetery: ADDLESTONE BURIAL GROUND, Surrey, United Kingdom

MANSER, Victor George
Private 10939, 1st Bn. East Surrey Regiment
Born in Hammersmith, 1896
Son of George and Elizabeth Ada Constance Manser, née Hall, of "Lynwood", High Street, Addlestone (m.1894)
Died of wounds, 19 November 1915, 1st Canadian General Hospital, Etaples, France, age 19
Cemetery: ETAPLES MILITARY CEMETERY, Pas de Calais, France

MASTERS, Percy
Driver 15362, 3rd Div. Ammunition Col., Royal Field Artillery
Born in Compton, West Sussex, 1878
Son of Peter Robert and Rhoda Masters, née Chalwin (d.1883); husband of Alice Le Gault (formerly Masters, née Abinett, of Pennywood, Yalding, Kent (m.1911); brother of Frederick George Masters, of Addlestone Moor (1911 census)

Died of wounds, 11 April 1917, France, age 38
Cemetery: DUISSANS BRITISH CEMETERY, ETRUN, Pas de Calais, France

MATTHEWS, Harold Edward
Gunner 164101, 146th Heavy Bty., Royal Garrison Artillery
Born in Ottershaw, 11 February 1882
Son of John and Rosetta Matthews, née Underwood, of Ottershaw (1911 census);
husband of Louisa Elizabeth Matthews, née Parsons, of Cowper Street, Hove, Sussex
(m.1906)
Died of wounds, 30 October 1917, Belgium, age 35
Cemetery: LIJSSENTHOEK MILITARY CEMETERY, Poperinge, West Vlaanderen,
Belgium

MILES, Alfred George
Private 10819, 5th Bn. Dorsetshire Regiment
Born in Chertsey, 1892
Baptised, 5 June 1892, St Paul's, Addlestone
Eldest son of Henry and Alice Miles, née Baigent, of Australian Cottages, Woodham
Lane, New Haw, Addlestone (m.1891); cousin of Charles Edwin Miles and William
Henry Miles; also fatal casualties
Killed in action, 26 September 1916, France, while taking part in an attack near Mouquet
Farm, during the Battle of the Somme, age 24
Cemetery: POZIERES BRITISH CEMETERY, OVILLERS-LA BOISSELLE, Somme,
France

*'After being reported missing twelve months ago, Mr. and Mrs. H. Miles, of 2,
Australian Cottages, New Haw, have received information from the War Office that their
eldest son, Pte. Alfred G. Miles, of the Dorset Regt., was killed on the 26th September,
1916. Deceased was 24 years of age. He joined up the first month of war, and after
serving in the Dardanelles campaign and in Egypt he was brought back to France only a
couple of months before being killed. Prior to enlistment he was employed on the Wey
Manor golf course for several years. Mr. and Mrs. H. Miles have another son serving in
the Royal Navy and a foster son in Egypt, serving with the H.L.I.' (The Surrey Herald,
September 7, 1917)*

MILES, Charles Edwin
Private 25526, 2nd Bn. Duke of Wellington's (West Riding Regiment)
Enlisted, 4 September 1914
Born in Addlestone, 1895
Baptised, 11 August 1895, St Paul's, Addlestone
Son of Edward and Sarah Ann Miles, née Seward, of Woodbine
Cottages, Woodham Lane, New Haw, Addlestone (m.1879); cousin of
Alfred George Miles, also a fatal casualty
Killed in action, 30 August 1918, France, while taking part in an attack
near Haucourt, age 23
Cemetery: VIS-EN-ARTOIS BRITISH CEMETERY, HAUCOURT, Pas de Calais,
France

*'Pte. Charles Edwin Miles, of the Duke of Wellington's Regt., and son of Mrs. E. Miles,
of 2, Woodbine Cottages, New Haw, was killed in action on Aug. 30th. The deceased was
the fourth son of Mrs Miles, and the second to make the supreme sacrifice. His eldest*

brother, Pte. W.H. Miles, was wounded at Neuve Chapelle on March 12, 1915, and died of wounds on March 26th.

Pte. C.E. Miles enlisted on Sept. 4, 1914, and was drafted out to France within a week of being sworn in as a driver in the A.S.C., in which capacity he served for three years. He was out in France for 17 months without home leave, his second and last leave being in August of 1917. He was transferred from the A.S.C. and trained for the infantry, and then drafted to the Duke of Wellington's Regt. At the time of his death he was 23 years old. Mrs. Miles has two sons-in-law still serving, both of whom have been wounded.' (The Surrey Herald, September 20, 1918)

MILES, William Henry

Private 2063, 2nd Bn. East Surrey Regiment
Born in Addlestone, 1884
Baptised, 30 November 1884, St Paul's, Addlestone
Eldest son of Edward and Sarah Ann Miles, née Seward, of
Woodbine Cottages, Woodham Lane, New Haw, Addlestone
(m.1879); husband of Ethel Bailey, formerly Miles, née Cheeseman
(m.22 August 1908, St Paul's, Addlestone); cousin of Alfred George
Miles, also a fatal casualty
Died, 26 March 1915, at 3rd London General Hospital, Wandsworth,
from wounds received during an engagement near Spanbroekmolen,
Belgium, on 12 March 1915, some 20 km north of Neuve Chapelle, age 30
Cemetery: WANDSWORTH (EARLSFIELD) CEMETERY, London, United Kingdom

'Our readers will learn with regret of the death of Pte. William H. Miles, of the 2nd East Surrey Regiment. It is believed that he was wounded at Neuve Chapelle, although accurate information is not yet to hand.

Pte. Miles, who was in his 30th year, was the son of Mrs. E. Miles, of Woodham Road, New Haw, and he had joined the Services for the duration of war. He was previously employed as greensman at St. George's Hills. He had lived in Addlestone all his life, and married Miss Ethel Cheeseman, whose parents live in Station Road, Addlestone, and had two little children. Four of his brothers are with the Army, including one at the Front, and a brother-in-law is also on active service. Our readers will remember that some weeks back Mrs. Miles received a congratulatory letter from the King, on being the mother of such a patriotic family.

Pte. Miles was wounded in the left foot and thigh with shrapnel, and he also received a gunshot wound over the right ear. An abscess formed over this, and when it was being removed it was discovered that the shrapnel had penetrated to the brain. He was brought over to England and taken to the 3rd London General Hospital, where he received the most careful attention possible. The hospital ship in which he was conveyed was attacked by a German submarine whilst in the Channel, but managed to escape.

Pte. Miles told his mother whilst he was lying in hospital that the scene of the fighting was a veritable hell. He mentioned one man, who stood next to him on one occasion, who was blown to pieces, and parts of his flesh were scattered in all directions.

The end came early on Friday morning. Although the poor fellow was full of agony he never once murmured, and almost the last words to his wife were that he was going home soon. The funeral took place at the Wandsworth Cemetery on Monday, when the body of Pte. Miles was accorded full military honours.' (The Surrey Herald, April 2, 1915)

NEW, Edward

Private G/18065, 8th Bn. Queen's (Royal West Surrey Regiment)
Born in Addlestone, 2 October 1886
Baptised, 3 November 1886, St Paul's Addlestone
Son of John New of Flemish Fields, Chertsey (1911 census) and Mary Jane New, née
Willougby, (d.1887); husband of Edith Alice New, née Cooper, of Chapel Grove,
Addlestone (m.1910)
Killed in action, 31 July 1917, Belgium, while taking part in an attack at Pilckem Ridge
during the 3rd Battle of Ypres (Passchendaele), age 30
Memorial: YPRES (MENIN GATE) MEMORIAL, Ieper, West-Vlaanderen, Belgium

*'On Tuesday morning Mrs. New, of 51, Chapel Grove, received an official notification
from the Hounslow Record Office stating that her husband, Pte. Edward New, of the
Queen's R.W. Surrey Regt., had been killed in action on the 31st July.*

*The deceased was the son of Mr. John New, of Chertsey. He had served about eight
months in the fighting area, after joining the Forces during July, 1916. He was well-
known in the district, being a native of Addlestone, and was employed by the Addlestone
Co-operative Society prior to enlisting.' (The Surrey Herald, August 24, 1917)*

NOAKES, Albert Thomas

Private 1713A, 24th Bn. Australian Infantry, Australian Imperial Force
Enlisted, 30 April 1915
Moved to Australia, about 1913; worked as a farmhand in Portarlington, nr. Melbourne,
Victoria
Born in Badshot Lea, nr. Farnham, 1894
Son of Thomas and Mary Ann Noakes, née Bellinger, of Byron Lodge, Addlestone;
brother of Nelson William Noakes, 29th Bn. Australian Infantry, who died on the same
day
Killed in action, 28 July 1916, during the Battle of the Somme, while occupying trenches
in the Pozieres sector, age 22
Cemetery: SERRE ROAD CEMETERY No.2, Somme, France

*'I knew him personally, he was a great friend of mine. He was in B. Coy. No.7 Platoon.
We went into Kay's Sap, Pozieres, on 26th July, 1916. Next day, when the Germans were
bombing us very heavily, one of the shells which burst in the trench badly wounded
Noakes and others. I saw him and several others lying wounded in the trench. He was so
badly hurt that he could not move. They were doing all they could for the wounded but the
stretcher bearers were so very badly knocked about themselves that but little could be
done for them then. I did not see Noakes again but I am morally certain that he could not
have survived. We left that Sap the following night.' (Testimony of L/Cpl. W. H. Marshal.
Courtesy of the Australian Red Cross Society's Wounded and Missing Bureau)*

'THIRTEEN YEARS AFTERWARDS
*Mr. T. Noakes, of Brighton Road, Addlestone, has received a communication from
Australia House, London, which makes clear the fate of his son, Albert T. Noakes, of the
Australian Imperial Forces, who was presumed killed on July 27th, 1916, in France. He
went into action on that date with his company, all of whom were annihilated, and
nothing more was heard of them.*

*The communication states that during the recent operations of the Imperial War Graves
Commission the remains were found and identified. They forwarded deceased's title*

(badge), fountain pen, pipe, and knife, and added that the reburial took place in the Serre Road Cemetery, No.2.

Deceased and his two brothers enlisted in the Australian Forces at the commencement of the war. One of the other brothers was killed and the third, Capt. F.C. Noakes, is now in the Royal Engineers, stationed in Cairo.' (The Surrey Herald, May 10, 1929)

NOAKES, Nelson William

Private 1014, 29th Bn. Australian Infantry, Australian Imperial Force
Enlisted, 29 July 1915
Moved to Australia, 1913; worked as a farmhand in Portarlington, nr. Melbourne, Victoria
Born in Badshot Lea, nr. Farnham, 1896
Son of Thomas and Mary Ann Noakes, née Bellinger, of Byron Lodge, Addlestone; brother of Albert Thomas Noakes, 24th Bn. Australian Infantry, who died on the same day
Died, 28 July 1916, at 13th General Hospital, France, from wounds received on 19 July 1916, during an attack at Fromelles by the 5th Australian Division (Battle of the Somme), age 19
Cemetery: BOULOGNE EASTERN CEMETERY, Pas de Calais, France
(Photograph: courtesy of the Australian War Memorial)

'Mr. and Mrs. T. Noakes, of Brighton Road, have received the sad intelligence that their youngest son, Pte. N. Noakes, of the 29th Australian Battalion, passed away in a Boulogne hospital on Thursday last. Mention was made in our columns last week to the effect that the young fellow had been severely wounded in the shoulder and neck by shrapnel. He went to Australia about three years ago, but similarly to his brothers, Lieut. F. Noakes, Royal Engineers, and Sergt. Bert Noakes, 24th Australian Battalion, joined up soon after the declaration of war.' (The Surrey Herald, August 4, 1916)

O'FARRELL, Joseph Francis

Corporal 706, VII Corps, Cyclist Bn. Army Cyclist Corps
Born in Egham, 28 April 1886
Son of Thomas O'Farrell (d.1904) and Lucy Ellen O'Farrell, née Crampton; husband of Mary O'Farrell, née Wallace, of Cherry Tree Cottage, Ottershaw (m.1913)
Killed in action, 12 September 1917, France, age 31
Cemetery: FAVREUIL BRITISH CEMETERY, Pas de Calais, France

'With great regret we have to chronicle the death in action, in France, on the 12th September, of Cpl. J. O'Farrell, of the Cyclists Corps, whose wife resides at Cherry Tree Cottage, Ottershaw.

Cpl. O'Farrell was formerly employed by Mr. Cannon, contractor, of Addlestone, but he enlisted on the outbreak of war and crossed overseas some 26 months ago. It was only about a fortnight previously to his death that he was home with his wife and two children, enjoying a brief respite from the Front. He was 31 years of age. The sad intimation reached the widow by letters from several officers.

Extracts from letters received by the widow are appended:-

"He was with me on a detachment during the greater part of last winter, and was one of the finest N.C.O's I have ever known. He was greatly and universally beloved by the whole unit, and will be very much missed. It must be a great consolation to you to know that he died the finest death a man could have – for his King and country, and doing his

duty nobly. I am arranging for a cross to be erected over his grave at an early date, and we were able to bury him with full military honours. – Lieut. and Adjut. Tilly."

"It is with the greatest regret that I have to inform you of the death of your loving husband. He was killed in action on the morning of Sept. 12th, 1917, and fortunately he suffered no pain whatever, as he never regained consciousness after being hit. The funeral took place on the afternoon of the 12th Sept., when he was buried with full military honours, the service being witnessed by all his comrades. I need hardly suggest that your husband will be missed very much, as he was a great favourite amongst all officers and men of the Battalion. I shall miss him more than I can tell you, as I have been his officer now for over 12 months, and he was one of my best N.C.O's. I am enclosing a letter he wrote the night before he was killed, also his cap badge, which I thought you would like to have. Words cannot express my regret for you and your dear children." – Lieut. Jones.

"His death was instantaneous, and he would suffer no pain whatever. I feel that any words by me will be poor consolation for your bereavement, but I can assure you that you have the sincere sympathy of us all. Your husband has been with me now for over a year, and I have always reckoned on him as a good soldier, and a most reliable man in every way. Our hearts go out in sympathy for yourself and the little one." – Major J. Tennant. (The Surrey Herald, September 21, 1917)

O'FARRELL, Thomas

Corporal 32784, 14th Bn. Hampshire Regiment
Born in Egham, 1883
Son of Thomas O'Farrell (d.1904) and Lucy Ellen O'Farrell, née Crampton; husband of Henrietta Jane O'Farrell, née Hall, of Bury Farm Cottage, Hatch Bridge, Addlestone (m.1915)
Killed in action, 17 September 1917, France & Flanders, age 34
Memorial: TYNE COT MEMORIAL, Zonnebeke, West-Vlaanderen, Belgium

'It is with great regret that we have to record the death in France of another member of the O'Farrell family – Cpl. Thomas O'Farrell, of the Hampshire Regt., who fell on Sept. 17th. His wife resides at Cherry Tree Cottage, Ottershaw, and he was the second son of Mrs. White, of Wheatash-road. It will be recalled that we recently recorded the death of his younger brother, Cpl. J. O'Farrell, of the Cyclists Corps, who was killed on Sept. 12th. It will be seen that in less than a week both brothers made the supreme sacrifice.

Mrs. O'Farrell received the official intimation from the War Office on Saturday, informing her that her husband had been killed on the 17th of last month.

The deceased Corporal was 34 years of age. He joined up with the Regular Forces about 12 months before the outbreak of the Boer War. He passed through the South African campaign, gaining the S.A. medal and five bars. He remained in Africa for three years, then came to England and was granted his discharge. He later joined up with the Hampshire Regt., and went to Africa for another seven years. He returned to England five years ago last January. On the outbreak of the present war he was drafted to France with the original Expeditionary Force. In November, 1914, he was poisoned by water, this necessitating him returning to England. He crossed overseas again in the following February, but was gassed in April, 1915. Cpl. O'Farrell was then in hospital in France until November. He was then granted his discharge as a time expired man. Up to November, 1916, he was employed by Messrs. Gordon Watney and Co., Ltd., and he was then recalled to the Colours. He rejoined the Hampshires, and was again in the fighting area by June of the present year.' (The Surrey Herald, October 12, 1917)

OWEN, John Edward
Private 2427, 9th Bn. East Surrey Regiment
Born in Pendleton, Lancs, 1879
Son of Roderick (d.1896) and Jane Owen, of Manchester; husband of Mary Owen, née Eacott, of Liberty Hall Road, Addlestone (m.1904)
Died of wounds, 9 March 1916, France, age 36
Cemetery: LE TOUQUET-PARIS PLAGE COMMUNAL CEMETERY, Pas de Calais, France

'The sad news has been received by Mrs. Owen, of Liberty Hall-road, Addlestone, that her husband, Pte. John Edward Owen, of the 9th East Surrey Regt., has succumbed to wounds received in France.

The official War Office notification states that Pte. Owen died in a French hospital on March 10th. The deceased soldier, who was 36 years of age, enlisted as early as September, 1914, and went to France in August, 1915. After seven months strenuous service in France, Pte. Owen received his fatal wound. He leaves a wife and five children to mourn their loss, with whom great sympathy will be felt in their great bereavement.' (The Surrey Herald, April 7, 1916)

PERRY, Walter
Private 1115, 1st Bn. East Surrey Regiment
Enlisted in Kingston
Born in Addlestone (*Haddlestone*, Soldiers Died in the Great War), date unknown
Killed in action, 23 July 1916, France, during an attack by his battalion on the village of Longueval, during the Battle of the Somme
Memorial: THIEPVAL MEMORIAL, Somme, France

PLOWMAN, Samuel
Sergeant 4354, 9th Bn. East Surrey Regiment
Born in Addlestone, 1886
Baptised, 21 March 1886, St Paul's, Addlestone
Son of Hillel and Mary Plowman, née Brown, of Brighton Road, Addlestone (1901 census); husband of Helen Nellie Plowman, née Fowler, of Rose Lane, Ripley (m.1909)
Killed in action, 26 September 1915, France, on the second day of the Battle of Loos, while taking part in the unsuccessful attack by 24th Division in the vicinity of Hulluch, age 29
Memorial: LOOS MEMORIAL, Pas de Calais, France

POOK, Harold Alfred
Private 228019, 1st (City of London) Bn. London Regiment (Royal Fusiliers)
Born in Weybridge, 1897
Son of James Doddridge and Florence Pook, née Humphreys, of "Sunnymead", Woodham Lane, New Haw, Addlestone (1911 census)
Killed in action, 3 May 1917, France, while taking part in an abortive night attack on enemy trenches in the vicinity of Arras, age 20
Memorial: ARRAS MEMORIAL, Pas de Calais, France

'Mr. J.D. Pook of Sunnymede, New Haw, is most anxious to obtain further news of his son, Pte. Harold Alfred Pook, Royal Fusiliers (late of the 4th Royal Sussex Regt.), who was posted as missing after an engagement in France on May 3rd. The father, in asking our co-operation, says he hopes by the publicity to obtain some definite news, "seeing that your paper is so widely read, both at home and at the Front." Anyone hearing any tidings of Pte. Pook is asked to communicate with the parents.' (The Surrey Herald, June 8, 1917)

PROCTOR, Lewis Herman

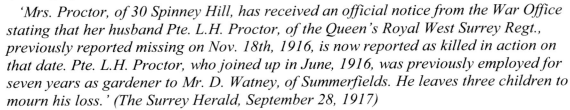

Private G/13944, 7th Bn. Queen's (Royal West Surrey Regiment)
Born in Long Marston, Herts., 1880
Son of John and Emma Proctor, of Long Marston, Tring, Herts;
husband of Ethel Ann Proctor, née Chandler, of Spinney Hill,
Addlestone (m.1905)
Killed in action, 18 November 1916, France, on the last day of the
Battle of the Somme, while taking part in an unsuccessful attack
towards the village of Grandcourt, age 36
Cemetery: GRANDCOURT ROAD CEMETERY, GRANDCOURT, Somme, France
(Photograph: courtesy of Mrs J Seaman)

'Mrs. Proctor, of 30 Spinney Hill, has received an official notice from the War Office stating that her husband Pte. L.H. Proctor, of the Queen's Royal West Surrey Regt., previously reported missing on Nov. 18th, 1916, is now reported as killed in action on that date. Pte. L.H. Proctor, who joined up in June, 1916, was previously employed for seven years as gardener to Mr. D. Watney, of Summerfields. He leaves three children to mourn his loss.' (The Surrey Herald, September 28, 1917)

RIGBY, Charles

Private S4/056878, 244th Coy. Supply Section, Army Service Corps
Born in Stamford Hill, Tottenham, 1886
Baptised, 12 September 1886, All Souls, Clapton Park
Son of Charles Rigby and Mrs Fanny Hollocks, formerly Rigby, née Davison (m.1880) of
Victoria Road, Addlestone (1911 census); husband of Ellen Margaret Rigby, née
Holloway of Radnor Road, Weybridge (m.1910) (1911 census)
Killed in action, 1 August 1915, Gallipoli Peninsula, Turkey, age 29
Cemetery: LANCASHIRE LANDING CEMETERY, Turkey

ROBERTS, Charles Henry

Private 29942, 2nd Bn. Royal Warwickshire Regiment
Born in Ecton Road, Addlestone, 1897
Baptised, 2 July 1897, St Paul's, Addlestone
Son of Charles Henry (d.1913) and Clara Roberts, née Edwards, of Thames Street,
Weybridge (m.1895); previously of Alexandra Road, Addlestone
Killed in action, 3 September 1916, France, during the Battle of the Somme, while taking
part in an attack near Ginchy, age 19
Memorial: THIEPVAL MEMORIAL, Somme, France

ROBERTS, John

Leading Stoker K/13658, H.M.S. *Queen Mary*, Royal Navy
Born in Addlestone, 1893
Son of John and Annie Elizabeth Roberts, née Simmons, of Rose
Cottage, Victoria Road, Addlestone (m.1888)
Died, 31 May 1916, on H.M.S. *Queen Mary*, a Dreadnought battlecruiser
of 26,270 tons. The ship was destroyed by magazine explosions after
direct hits by German battlecruisers during the Battle of Jutland. 1,266
officers and men were lost, 20 survived. Age 23
Memorial: PORTSMOUTH NAVAL MEMORIAL, Hampshire, United Kingdom

*'So far as is yet known, the only Addlestonian to fall victim to the Germans in the Battle
of Jutland was Chief Stoker J. Roberts, whose parents reside at Rose Cottage, Victoria-
road.*

*The deceased, who joined the Navy four years ago, and was only 23 years of age, had
been on the Queen Mary since that vessel was launched, and therefore took part in the
Battle of Heligoland.*

*An official intimation to the effect that Roberts was among the missing was received
from the Admiralty on Wednesday morning.*

*Mr. and Mrs. Roberts desire to return their heartfelt thanks to the many persons who
have expressed sympathy with them in the loss of their only son.' (The Surrey Herald,
June 9, 1916)*

ROGERS, William Reginald

Corporal G/4203, 1st Bn. Queen's (Royal West Surrey Regiment)
Enlisted in Addlestone (resident 1911 census)
Born in Chingford, 1890
Son of William Evans and Annie Rogers, née Tyler, of Hill House, Newhaven, Sussex
(m.1889)
Died of wounds, 23 August 1915, France, age 24
Cemetery: BETHUNE TOWN CEMETERY, Pas de Calais, France

ROSHIER, William George

Rifleman 592964, 2/18th (County of London) Bn. London Regiment
(London Irish Rifles)
Formerly 80189, R.A.M.C
Born in Lyne, Surrey, 1892
Son of William and Alice Roshier, of Lyne (1911 census); husband of
Charlotte Caroline Roshier, née Hiley, of Alexandra Road, Addlestone
(m.1914)
Killed in action, 23 December 1917, during Allenby's campaign in
Palestine, age 25
Memorial: JERUSALEM MEMORIAL, Israel

*'Mrs. W. G. Roshier, of 7, Factory Cottages, Alexandra-road, on Saturday learned that
her husband, Rifleman W. G. Roshier, of the London Regt., had been posted as missing
since the fighting in Egypt on the 23rd December.*

*Pte. Roshier was employed by Mr. W. G. Tarrant, of Byfleet, previously to enlisting
early in 1916. He crossed to France in June of the same year. Since that time he has seen
service in Salonica and Egypt.' (The Surrey Herald, January 25, 1918)*

SANDS, Henry

Private 240110, 1/6th East Surrey Regiment
Born in Addlestone, 1895
Baptised, 11 September 1895, St Paul's, Addlestone
3rd son of Joseph and Martha Ann Sands, née Preece, of Rydal Lodge, High Street,
Addlestone (m.1876)
Killed in action, 31 December 1916, Mesopotamia, while attached to the Norfolk
Regiment, age 21
Memorial: BASRA MEMORIAL, Iraq

'An official intimation reached Mr. and Mrs. Sands, of Rydal Lodge, High-street, a few days since that their son, Pte. H. Sands, of the 6th Battalion East Surrey Regiment, had been slightly wounded during the battle with the Turks at Ctesiphon on November 22nd. So far no actual details of the wound have reached the parents.

Pte. H. Sands was serving with the Chertsey Company of Territorials when war was declared, and he left with the Battalion for India, subsequently being one of the local men to volunteer for active service in the Persian Gulf operations. Prior to the war he was employed at the Leather Factory.' (The Surrey Herald, January 7, 1916)

'There is still no definite information concerning Pte. H. Sands, the local Territorial who went to India with the 6th East Surreys and subsequently to Mesopotamia, and who is known to have been wounded at the Battle of Ctesiphon. The last letter which has reached his anxious parents from Pte. Sands personally was dated November 7th, or nearly eight months ago. In response to inquiries, the officials at the Record Office have intimated to the parents that their son is "presumed" to be a prisoner of war with the Turks, following the fall of Kut-el-Amara.' (The Surrey Herald, June 23, 1916)

'Mr. and Mrs. Sands, of Rydal Lodge, have received the gift which their son, Pte. Harry Sands, of the Chertsey Territorials, was supposed to have received at Christmas, 1914, from Princess Mary. Within the brass box was a bullet pencil and a card of greeting for the New Year of 1915. Pte. Sands left India for Mesopotamia, and was in Kut. His parents have not heard from him since November 7th, 1915, but the authorities still presume him to be a prisoner.' (The Surrey Herald, October 27, 1916)

SCHUMACHER, Samuel

Private 38727, 14th Bn. (West of England) Gloucestershire Regiment
Born in Limerick, Ireland, 1887
Son of John and Agnes Schumacher, of Kilfinane, Co. Limerick;
husband of Martha Ellen Schumacher, née Oke, of Eastworth Road,
Chertsey (m. 25 December 1915, St Paul's, Addlestone)
Died, 16 September 1918, POW in Germany, age 31
Cemetery: COLOGNE SOUTHERN CEMETERY, Koln (Cologne),
Nordrhein-Westfal, Germany
Photograph: courtesy of Chertsey Museum

'The sad news reached Mrs. Schumacher, of Eastworth-road, on Tuesday morning that her husband – Pte. S. Schumacher of the 14th Gloucesters – had died whilst a prisoner-of-war in Germany. The deceased was captured on March 23rd of last year, and comrades since liberated have written to the effect that for some time afterwards he was engaged in loading shells behind the German lines. During the autumn he was taken ill and put in a train bound for Germany, but the following day he was removed and taken to

another hospital. Some months have elapsed since his wife heard directly from him, and the letter she received on Tuesday stated that he died in the hospital referred to.

For many years Pte. Schumacher was butler to Sir Albert K. Rollit, of St Ann's Hill, and he married a daughter of Mr. C. Oake, of Eastworth-road. The greatest sympathy will be extended to the widow, who received such sad information when thousands of other prisoners-of-war are being liberated.' (The Surrey Herald, January 10, 1919)

SHUTTLE, George James Henry

Ordinary Seaman J/41530, H.M.S. *Pembroke*, Royal Navy
Enlisted, 12 July 1917
Born in Brentford, Middlesex, 12 July 1899
Baptised, 4 August 1899, St George's, Old Brentford
Son of Ellen Shuttle (b.1879); grandson of Henry Edwin (d. 1899) and Maria Shuttle, née Swift of Chapel Park Road, Addlestone (1901 census); adopted son of Noah and Caroline Scott of Row Town, Addlestone (1911 census)
Died, 4 September 1917, from wounds received at 11.12 on the previous evening when German Gotha aircraft bombed the Medway Towns of Kent, including the drill hall of H.M.S. Pembroke - the Royal Naval Barracks in Chatham. The drill hall was in use as sleeping accommodation and suffered a direct hit. The bomb shattered the glass roof and exploded on the floor, sending shards of glass on those sleeping below. 135 servicemen died as a result of the attack - the largest single loss of life from an air raid in the UK during the war. Age 18
Cemetery: GILLINGHAM (WOODLANDS) CEMETERY, Kent, United Kingdom

SIZMUR, William Herbert

Private L/8254, 1st Bn. Queen's (Royal West Surrey) Regiment
Born in Ottershaw, 1888
Baptised, 4 November 1888, Christchurch, Ottershaw
Son of Alfred and Eliza Sizmur, née Mant, of Furze Road, Hare Hill, Chertsey (m.1885)
Died, 13 October 1914, at Paignton Hospital, from wounds received near Mons, Belgium, age 26
Cemetery: ADDLESTONE BURIAL GROUND, Surrey, United Kingdom

'It is with great regret that we record the death of Pte. W. Sizmur, of the West Surrey Regiment, whose home was at Ottershaw. Last week we reported that he had been wounded in the back by shrapnel, and had lost the use of both legs. He was then in Paignton Hospital. Despite every effort to save his life, he died on Tuesday afternoon from the effects of the wound.' (The Surrey Herald, October 16, 1914)

'FUNERAL OF PTE. SIZMUR
It is easy to be patriotic when everything goes along nicely, but when those who are dear to us go under in the war the tragedy of it is a very real one. Pte. W. Sizmur, of the West Surrey Regiment, a son of Mr. A. Sizmur, of Hare Hill, has given his life for his country, having died of shrapnel wounds, and was buried at Addlestone Cemetery on Sunday afternoon. With the Addlestone Band, the procession started on foot from the house at Hare Hill, the Dead March in "Saul" being played.

The coffin was conveyed on a bier. When passing the Parish Church "Abide with me" was given. At the Cemetery there was a large crowd of sympathisers, the impressive service being conducted by the Vicar (the Rev. A. Cuming). The last honours were paid by members of the National Reserve, who acted as the firing party.

The inscription on the coffin was: "Pte. W. Sizmur, 2nd Battalion R.W.S. age 27. He died for King and Country." Nearly sixty beautiful floral tributes were placed on and around the grave.

Failing a funeral with honours carried out by a military party, the Addlestone Co. of the National Reserve felt it their duty and privilege to show all respect and honour to the first village lad who has fallen in duty for his country.

The arrangements were made by Pte. H. Elms. The parade was in charge of Sergt. P. Maytum and a full firing party under the direction of Corpl. Buckler fired the three volleys, while the last post was sounded by three buglers. The Addlestone Band gave their services willingly, under the baton of Bandmaster Hawkins.

The family desire to sincerely thank the many persons who expressed sympathy or forwarded flowers.' (The Surrey Herald, October 23, 1914)

'LOCAL PERSONS BEAR COST OF BURIAL

It may not be generally known that when a soldier who has been wounded at the front succumbs in this country, the military authorities bear the expenses of burial in the town where the poor fellow passes away. Consequently if another place of burial is desired by the relatives, they must bear the expenses incurred in interring the body.

It cost £9 to convey the body of Pte. Sizmur, of the Queen's Regiment, from Paignton Hospital to Hare Hill, and several local persons considered that the parents should not bear this financial burden in addition to their sorrow. Two sections have been collecting, as Mr. Harris made a collection at Hare Hill and Ottershaw, and three or four Addlestone tradesmen formed themselves into a Committee to obtain subscriptions in Addlestone.

The response was very gratifying. The Addlestone tradesmen collected £9, and so handed the parents the receipted account. Mr. Harris succeeded in getting together £5 5s.7d., which sum he handed to the parents.

The members of the Committee desire to tender their thanks for the kind and generous support accorded their efforts, and the parents of the deceased soldier hope that the subscribers and the collectors will accept this intimation of their gratitude.' (The Surrey Herald, November 6, 1914)

SKEATS, George Walter

Private 9616, 5th Bn. Duke of Edinburgh's (Wiltshire Regiment)
Born in Addlestone, 1891
Baptised, 24 April 1891, St Paul's, Addlestone
Son of William and Harriett Ada Skeats, née Watts, of Victoria Road, Addlestone (1911 census) (m.1881)
Died, 5 February 1919, Kings College Hospital, Denmark Hill, London SE, from a bullet wound in the thigh, received on 9 August 1915 at Chunuk Bair, Gallipoli Peninsula, age 27
Cemetery: ADDLESTONE BURIAL GROUND, Surrey, United Kingdom

'Lance-Corpl. G.W. Skeats, of the Wilts. Regt., whose home is in the Victoria Road, was wounded in the leg at the Dardanelles on August 9th, and is now in Cairo Hospital. He was employed at the Linoleum Factory before he joined up.' (The Surrey Herald, September 3, 1915)

'Pte. Skeats has reached a London hospital from Alexandria. He is paralysed in several limbs, and his throat is also affected.' (The Surrey Herald, September 13, 1918)

'The deepest sympathy is extended to Mrs. Skeats, of 38, Victoria-road, on the death of her youngest son, George, aged 27 years, who died in a hospital at Denmark Hill on Feb. 5th, after a long illness and much pain, which was most bravely borne. The deceased was brought home from Egypt last October, having previously served with the 5th Wilts. Regt., which went to Gallipoli, where he was wounded. The body was interred at Addlestone on Tuesday.

The deepest gratitude is extended to the sisters and nurses of the hospital, who by their devotion succeeded in making his last days happy. One of the nurses has written to deceased's sister:

"I have been with your brother since he first came in, and a sweeter and more lovable patient to nurse one could not find. His character and personality will always be a beautiful memory to me all my life. If he had lived he would only have had to suffer infinitely more. So it is our one consolation that he passed away before he had to suffer what would have been his lot later on. His courage and cheerfulness was wonderful. And I'm so glad he had all the pleasure which he was able to enjoy during the last two or three months. We can only try and find solace in the thought that he is happy now." (The Surrey Herald, February 14, 1919)

SMITHERS, Henry Charles

Private L/11988, 2/4th Bn. Queen's (Royal West Surrey Regiment)
Born in Addlestone Moor, 1897
Baptised, 9 January 1898, St Paul's, Addlestone
Son of James Richard and Paulina Bertha Smithers, née Stoter, of Shaftesbury Villas, Addlestone Moor (m.1882)
Killed in action, 29 July 1918, France, during the Battles of the Marne and while taking part in an attack on the Grand Rozoy Ridge, age 20
Cemetery: RAPERIE BRITISH CEMETERY, VILLEMONTOIRE, Aisne, France

SNOOK, Charles Albert

Private G/13248, 7th Bn. Buffs (East Kent Regiment)
Attested, 12 February 1916
Born in Barnes, 1895
Son of William Henry (d.1914) and Fanny Snook, née Gill, of Victoria Inn, Woodham Lane, Woodham, Addlestone (m.1877)
Died, 26 August 1918, from wounds received near Morlancourt, France, during the advance in Picardy, age 23
Awards: MILITARY MEDAL: Issue No. 31142, Sixth Supplement to the London Gazette, 21 January 1919, published 24 January 1919
Cemetery: ALBERT COMMUNAL CEMETERY EXTENSION, Somme, France

'HONOURS FOR SOLDIERS – PRESENTATION OF MEDALS – At the depot of The Queen's, Stoughton, Guildford, on Tuesday, Capt. R.C.G. Foster, M.C., at a special parade, presented medals to the following:-

Pte. C. Snook (the late), 7th Buffs, Victoria, Woodham-lane, West Byfleet, Military Medal, received by his mother.' (The Surrey Advertiser and County Times, May 3, 1919)

SPENCER, William John
Private G/8355, 7th Bn. Queen's (Royal West Surrey Regiment)
Born in Bethnel Green, 1876
Son of George and Elizabeth Spencer, of Pimlico, London; husband of Esther Spencer, née Fish, of Darton Road, Cawthorne, Barnsley; previously of Row Town, Addlestone (m.1903)
Killed in action, 28 September 1916, during the Battle of the Somme and while taking part in an attack towards the Schwaben Redoubt, near Thiepval, age 40
Cemetery: MILL ROAD CEMETERY, THIEPVAL, Somme, France

'An official intimation from the War Office reached Mrs. Spencer, of Rowhill, on Thursday morning of last week to the effect that her husband, Pte. W. J. Spencer, of the Queen's Royal West Surreys, had been killed in action on the 28th September, during the heavy fighting on the Somme.

Pte. Spencer, who was 39 years of age, enlisted during March of the present year, crossing to France on the 10th July. He had formerly been employed by Mr. Teesdale, of Franklands, as a butler, and had held this post for 7½ years before his enlistment. He was also an enthusiastic member of the Addlestone Volunteer Training Corps.

Pte. Spencer leaves a wife and five children.

Mrs Spencer wishes to thank the numerous friends for the sympathy shown to her in her great bereavement.' (The Surrey Herald, October 27, 1916)

SPONG, Alfred James
Lance Corporal L/10684, 8th Bn. Queen's (Royal West Surrey Regiment)
Born in Rowtown, Addlestone, 1895
Baptised, 24 November 1895, St Paul's, Addlestone
Son of William and Olive Spong, née Hyatt, (d.1914), of Row Town, Addlestone (m.1890)
Killed in action, 3 August 1917, near Ypres, Belgium, age 21
Memorial: YPRES (MENIN GATE) MEMORIAL, Ieper, West-Vlaanderen, Belgium

'Information has reached Mr. Wm. Spong, of Rowtown, that his second son, Lc.-Cpl. Alfred Spong, of the Queen's R.W. Surrey Regt. (machine gunner), has been killed in France.

Mr. Spong received the sad news by a letter from the Captain Commanding the deceased's Company. A letter has also reached the bereaved father from a comrade. Writing under date of the 3rd August, the Captain says: "I very much regret to have to inform you that during the recent operations your son was instantaneously killed by a machine gun bullet in the head. In some small measure I can share in your bereavement, as he had served under me for some time, and I was not only personally very fond of him but knew how popular he was with all his comrades. Believe me, that I sympathise with you very much in your loss, but it is hard to find any adequate words of comfort." The comrade's letter stated that the deceased was killed by a sniper's bullet in the head.

The late Lc.-Cpl. Spong was 21 years of age. Joining the Army on the outbreak of war, he crossed overseas in February, 1915. In August, 1916, he was wounded by shrapnel in the chest. He remained in England until March of this year. Prior to enlisting the deceased was employed by the late Mr. Howard, of Rowtown.

Mr. Spong's eldest son – Pte. W. Spong, also of the Queen's – is still in hospital suffering from a wound received in July, 1916. The third son is attached to the Royal Marine Artillery.' (The Surrey Herald, August 24, 1917)

SPONG, Frederick John

Gunner RMA/15675, H.M.S. *Resolution*, Royal Marine Artillery
Born in Rowtown, Addlestone, 4 November 1899
Baptised, 25 November 1899, St Paul's, Addlestone
Son of William and Olive Spong, née Hyatt, (d. 1914), of Row Town, Addlestone (m.1890)
Died of unspecified illness, 5 November 1918, on H.M.S. *Resolution*, age 19

H.M.S. Resolution was a 27,500 ton Dreadnought battleship in the Royal Sovereign Class; launched in January 1915, and broken up at Faslane in 1948
Cemetery: ADDLESTONE BURIAL GROUND, Surrey, United Kingdom

STEER, Reuben William

Driver T/440923, Royal Army Service Corps
Born in Addlestone, 1885
Baptised, 7 January 1886, St Paul's, Addlestone
Eldest son of Thomas and Elizabeth Jane Steer, née Mortimer, of Chapel Avenue, Addlestone (1911 census) (m.1882)
Died of influenza, 27 October 1918, Brook War Hospital, Kidbrooke, London SE, age 32
Cemetery: ADDLESTONE BURIAL GROUND, Surrey, United Kingdom

STEVENS, Frederick

Corporal G/5019, 9th Bn. Royal Sussex Regiment
Born in Easebourne, Sussex, 1881
Son of John and Hannah Stevens, née Greenwood, of Easebourne; husband of Kate Stevens, née Mills, of Crockford Park Road, Addlestone (1911 census) (m.1908)
Killed in action, 22 March 1918, France, on the second day of the German Spring Offensive, in the vicinity of St Quentin, age 37
Memorial: POZIERES MEMORIAL, Somme, France

'LOCAL CASUALTIES - The following names appear in the last official list of casualties: Killed, ...Corpl. F Stevens, Royal Sussex...' (The Surrey Herald, May 17, 1918)

STEVENS, Thomas Wilfred

Rifleman 572916, 2/17th (County of London) Bn. London Regiment (Poplar and Stepney Rifles)
Formerly, 72593 R.A.M.C.
Born in Addlestone, 1894
Son of Frederick and Hannah Stevens, née Linnegar, of Liberty Hall Road, Addlestone (m.1887)
Died of wounds, 1 May 1918, Palestine, age 23
Cemetery: JERUSALEM WAR CEMETERY, Israel

'Mr. and Mrs. Stevens, of Liberty Hall-road, have received the sad news of the death of their son, Rflm. T. W. Stevens, of the County of London Regt. Rflm. Stevens joined up in 1915, and he has seen two years overseas service. He proceeded to France from England, and has since served in Salonica, Egypt and Palestine, where he met his death on the 1st

May. Rflm. Stevens was one of those to enter Jerusalem with Gen. Allenby. Prior to enlisting he was employed by Mr. H. Tubb, butcher.' (The Surrey Herald, May 10, 1918)

STICKLEY, Herbert Alfred

Gunner 14490, A Bty. 93rd Bde. Royal Field Artillery
Born in Hagley, Worcs., 1895
Son of Herbert James and Rebecca Stickley, née Atkins (m.1889) of Row Town, Addlestone (1911 census); husband of Nellie Matilda Stickley, née Western, of Elgin Terrace, Maida Vale, London (m.18 July 1917, eight weeks before Herbert Alfred's death)
Died of wounds, 12 September 1917, Belgium, age 22
Cemetery: DOZINGHEM MILITARY CEMETERY, Poperinge, West-Vlaanderen, Belgium

SWEENEY, Patrick

Private 1000746, 27th Bn. Canadian Infantry (Manitoba Regiment)
Enlisted, 21 February 1916, Canadian Expeditionary Force
Sailed from Liverpool, 14 September 1912, SS Megantic, bound for Montreal
Born in Addlestone, 20 March 1891
Baptised, 11 June 1891, St Paul's, Addlestone
Son of Terence (d.1910) and Clara Sweeney, née Chapman, of Chapel Park, Addlestone (m.1880)
Killed in action, 6 November 1917, during the last phase of the Third Battle of Ypres (Passchendaele) and on the day when the 1st and 2nd Canadian Divisions finally captured the village of Passchendaele, age 26
Memorial: YPRES (MENIN GATE) MEMORIAL, Ieper, West-Vlaanderen, Belgium

'With deep regret we have to record the death in France, on the 6th November, of Pte. Patrick Sweeney, of the Canadian Scottish, and son of Mrs. Sweeney, of 39, Chapel Park.

The deceased soldier enlisted in Canada about two years ago, and had seen service in France for the past six months. Mrs. Sweeney received the sad news of her son's death in the form of letters from the Officer Commanding deceased's company and from a Corporal.

The officer has written: "Just a line to offer you the deepest sympathies of the officers and men of C Company. Your son was one of the best soldiers and the cheerfullest men we had in the Company, and we feel his loss most keenly. He met his death after we had attained our objective on the 6th inst. by a bursting shell. His death was instantaneous. Sweeney has been through several fights with me, and a braver boy never put on a uniform."

Cpl. J. W. Stephenson says: "I am very sorry indeed to inform you that your son was killed in action on the 6th November, by a shell exploding. He was killed instantly, and I can assure you that he never suffered any pain whatever. The officers, N.C.O's and men all send their deepest sympathy in the sad loss of your beloved son."

Mrs. Sweeney has three other sons serving in France. Lc.-Cpl. C. J. Sweeney, Royal Engineers, formerly of the East Surreys, has been wounded twice, and was in the Retreat from Mons. Pte. R. C. Sweeney, of the A.S.C. (M.T.), who joined on the outbreak of the war, and Pte. T. Sweeney, of the Gordon Highlanders, who has been wounded three times and buried by a shell.' (The Surrey Herald, December 7, 1917)

SYMES, Thomas Joel

Sergeant A/3425, 7th Bn. King's Royal Rifle Corps
Born in Addlestone, 2 August 1882
Son of Joel and Annie Elizabeth Clara Symes, née Banister, of Station Road, Addlestone (1911 census); husband of Harriett Lydia Symes, née Wakefield, of Darwin Road, South Ealing, London (m.1907)
Killed in action, 23 March 1918, near Pozieres, France, age 35
Memorial: POZIERES MEMORIAL, Somme, France

TALBOT, Joseph William

Lance Corporal 7058, Cavalry of the Line, 3rd (Prince of Wales's) Dragoon Guards
Born in Kensington, 31 December 1884
Son of Joseph William and Ellen Talbot, née Bloomfield, of Paddington, London (1911 census) (m.1884)
Killed in action, 2 June 1915, during a German attack near Hooge, age 30
Memorial: YPRES (MENIN GATE) MEMORIAL, Ieper, West-Vlaanderen, Belgium

'By means of a letter to his fiancée – Miss May, of Charlotte Villas, Addlestone Moor – the news has reached Addlestone of the death of a gallant Dragoon, in the person of Corpl. J. Talbot, 3rd Dragoon Guards, whose home is in Church Road, Addlestone. Both Corpl. Talbot and Miss May are well known in the locality and we are sure the sympathy of Addlestonians will go out to the lady in her great loss.

Details of the tragic affair are given in the following letter, sent by Sergt. T. H. Chalmers from Ypres on June 3rd:-

"Dear Miss May, - It is with the utmost regret that I take up a pencil to convey news which I am sure must mean a good deal of pain and sorrow to you.

No. 7005, Corpl. J. Talbot, 3rd Dragoon Guards, was killed in action yesterday whilst gallantly rescuing a wounded comrade.

Joe was one of my troop corporals and one of the best, not only was he under me for a good few years, but he was one of my best friends, and one I had utmost respect for. He was a real type of soldier, and his loss is keenly felt in my troop, particularly by myself.

Two of our men were on lookout during a very heavy bombardment. Suddenly a shell burst, killed one, and severely wounded the other. Joe, two others, and myself went out to try and get the fellow in, and whilst lifting him up another shell burst quite close, and poor Joe was killed right out. The shock of the explosion killed him and death was instantaneous, as there was not a wound on him.

At dark last night we buried him with two others of the troop, outside the trenches at Hooge village, erected a rough cross over them, and thus ended one of my best friends.

There is consolation in knowing a soldier's death is a noble one, and that is what we are all facing, and we never know when it is coming.

I am forwarding his diary on to you as he wished, and have taken the liberty of concluding the diary of a brave soldier, and at the same time one of my best friends.

Any other information I can give you can always be had, and I conclude by offering you my deepest sympathy, and by remaining ever yours, sincerely, T. H. Chalmers, Sergt., B. Squadron, 3rd Dragoon Guards." (The Surrey Herald, June 11, 1915)

TICKNER, Edward Albert

Private 240429, 12th Bn. East Surrey Regiment
Enlisted in Territorial Force, 25 November 1913
Born in Addlestone, 1895
Son of William John and Elizabeth Tickner, née Wilson (d.1909) of Pelican Lane, Hamm Moor, Weybridge
Killed in action, 4 June 1918, Belgium, age 23
Cemetery: HAGLE DUMP CEMETERY, Ieper, West-Vlaanderen, Belgium

'News has been received of the death, in action in France, of Pte. E. A. Tickner, of the East Surrey Regt., and second son of Mr. and Mrs. W. Tickner, Pelican-lane.' (The Surrey Herald, June 14, 1918)

TIMBLICK, Henry

Private L/9524, 1st Bn. Queen's (Royal West Surrey Regiment)
Enlisted, 16 February 1909
Born in Fulham, 26 January 1891
Son of Henry and Eliza Timblick, née Fulker, of Common Lane, New Haw (1911 Census) (m.1885)
Died, 30 October 1918, at 3rd Western General Hospital, Cardiff, from gas shell poisoning sustained in France, age 27
Cemetery: ADDLESTONE BURIAL GROUND, Surrey, United Kingdom

TULLIDGE, Bernard Henry

Captain, 6th Bn. attached 1/8th Bn. Worcestershire Regiment
Born in Newport, Isle of Wight, 28 September 1891
Baptised, 30 December 1891, St Thomas', Newport
Son of Henry (d.1919) and Amy Constance Tullidge, née Jupe (m.1888) (d.1957);
nephew of Emily Tullidge, wife of Rev. Edward Dennett, curate at Addlestone 1914-19
Killed in action, 27 August 1917, Belgium, Ypres Salient, near St Julien, during an attack through heavy mud, age 25
Memorial: TYNE COT MEMORIAL, Zonnebeke, West-Vlaanderen, Belgium

TULLIDGE, Robert Milton

Captain, 9th Bn. Royal Warwickshire Regiment
Born in Newport, Isle of Wight, 26 November 1892
Baptised, 1 March 1893, St Thomas', Newport
Son of Henry (d.1919) and Amy Constance Tullidge, née Jupe (m.1888) (d.1957);
nephew of Emily Tullidge, wife of Rev. Edward Dennett, curate at Addlestone 1914-19
Died of wounds, 25 January 1917, Mesopotamia, age 24
Cemetery: AMARA WAR CEMETERY, Iraq

TURNER, Arthur Walter

Driver 36412, 15th Field Coy., Royal Engineers
Enlisted, 20 April 1915
Born in Ottershaw, 1897
Baptised, 20 June 1897, St Paul's, Addlestone
7th son of Alfred and Jane Turner, née Bartram, of Common Lane, New Haw, Addlestone (1911 census) (m.1 November 1873)
Died of wounds, 29 January 1916, Cix Marechal, France, age 18

Cemetery: SAILLY-SUR-LA-LYS- CANADIAN CEMETERY, Pas de Calais, France

'The sympathy of our readers will assuredly go out to Mr. and Mrs. Turner, of Common Lane, Newhaw, Addlestone in the extraordinary toll the Great War has taken of their sons.

Few families in England can have made the supreme sacrifice for King and Country on three occasions, but such has been the case with Mr. and Mrs. Turner, who have just received official intimation that their youngest son, Driver A. W. Turner, of the Royal Engineers, has succumbed to wounds received in France on January 29th. The young fellow enlisted in February last year.

The retreat from Mons cost the family a son who was doing well in Britain's Regular Army. This was Sergt. E. Turner, of the 2nd East Surrey Regt., who had been in India for seven years previously to the outbreak of war, and who was 27 years of age – the eldest son.

Pte. B. Turner, the second son to succumb – for of that there is little doubt, although official information to this effect has not actually been received – enlisted a month after the clash of arms (September 1914). Going with the 5th Dorsets to the Gallipoli Peninsular, he was officially reported to have been wounded on August 21st. That was the last news concerning him, and as six months have transpired little hope is entertained that he is alive.

Mr. and Mrs. Turner's only other son is Pte. W. Turner, who enlisted in the R.A.M.C. four months ago and is now stationed at Longbridge.

The three brothers who have enlisted since war was declared were all in the employ of Mr. W. G. Tarrant, builder, of Byfleet.' (The Surrey Herald, February 11, 1916)

TURNER, Bertie

Private 10951, 5th Bn. Dorsetshire Regiment
Born in New Haw, 1893
Baptised, 7 May 1893, St Paul's, Addlestone
6th son of Alfred and Jane Turner, née Bartram, of Common Lane, New Haw, Addlestone (1911 census) (m.1 November 1873)
Killed in action, 21 August 1915, during the last major British attack of the Gallipoli campaign, age 22
Memorial: HELLES MEMORIAL, Turkey

TURNER, Ernest George

Sergeant 9513, 2nd Bn. East Surrey Regiment
Enlisted, 30 April 1908
Born in New Haw 1889
Baptised, 9 February 1890, St Paul's, Addlestone
4th son of Alfred and Jane Turner, née Bartram, of Common Lane, New Haw, Addlestone (1911 census) (m.1 November 1873)
Killed in action, 14 February 1915, near Ypres, Belgium, 26 days after his battalion landed in France from India via England, age 25
Memorial: YPRES (MENIN GATE) MEMORIAL, Ieper, West-Vlaanderen, Belgium

TURRELL, William Jesse

Private 37156, 9th Bn. Royal Fusiliers (City of London Regiment)
Born in Addlestone, 1885
Baptised, 28 October 1885, St Paul's, Addlestone
Son of John and Mary Turrell, of Albert Road, Addlestone
(1911 census); husband of Edith Kate Weeks (formerly Turrell, née
Smith, of Bryn Bank, Twyford, Winchester, (m.1915) (formerly of
Basingstoke Cottages, Common Lane, New Haw, Addlestone)
Killed in action, 3 May 1917, France, during the Allied Arras Offensive,
age 31
Memorial: ARRAS MEMORIAL, France

*'On Tuesday morning Mrs. Turrell, of Basingstoke Cottages, New Haw, received an
official War Office notice informing her that her husband, Pte. William T. Turrell, of the
Royal Fusiliers, had been posted as missing after an engagement on the 3rd May.*

*Pte. Turrell crossed to France last October, having enlisted the previous June. Prior to
joining the forces he had been employed for nine years by Messrs. T. G. Thomas and Son,
bootmakers, Weybridge.' (The Surrey Herald, June 8, 1917)*

WAKEFIELD, John Beauchamp

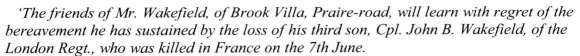

Corporal 373405, 1/8th (City of London) Bn. London Regiment (Post
Office Rifles)
Born in Ewell, Surrey, 1 March 1897
Son of Caleb and Eliza Alice Wakefield, née Wigmore (d.1907) of
Prairie Road, Addlestone (1911 census) (m.1881)
Killed in action, 7 June 1917, Belgium, on the first day of the Battle of
Messines, age 20
Memorial: YPRES (MENIN GATE) MEMORIAL, Ieper, West-
Vlaanderen, Belgium

*'The friends of Mr. Wakefield, of Brook Villa, Praire-road, will learn with regret of the
bereavement he has sustained by the loss of his third son, Cpl. John B. Wakefield, of the
London Regt., who was killed in France on the 7th June.*

*In addition to the War Office notification, Mr. Wakefield has received a number of
letters from the comrades of the deceased. A letter from a Lieut. is worded as follows. –
"I am writing on behalf of myself and the other officers of "C" company to express our
very deep sympathy with you in the loss of your son, Cpl. Wakefield, of the London
Regiment. He was a splendid fellow, and a most capable N.C.O., popular alike with
officers and men, and we are all deeply grieved at his death. As perhaps you knew for
some time before the action in which he was killed he had been doing more responsible
work than is usually performed by a corporal, and as there was no officer attached to his
platoon the whole of the work fell to him and his platoon sergeant. During this time he
showed the stuff he was made of and had he lived he would very soon have obtained
promotion."*

*The late Cpl. Wakefield, who was an old Tiffin's schoolboy, joined up at the age of 18,
and he had been in France since August, 1916. At the time of his death he was 20 years of
age. He was formerly employed by the L. & S.W. Railway at Waterloo Station.' (The
Surrey Herald, June 29, 1917)*

WATTS, William James

2nd Corporal 42035, 62nd Field Coy., Royal Engineers
Born in Addlestone, 15 April 1886
Baptised, 16 May 1886, St Paul's, Addlestone
Son of William and Ellen Watts, née Taylor, of Chapel Avenue,
Addlestone (1911 census) (m.1882)
Died, 9 May 1916, at Epsom Military Hospital, from gas poisoning,
age 30
Cemetery: ADDLESTONE BURIAL GROUND, Surrey, United Kingdom
Photograph: courtesy of Abigail Aish, great-niece of William James Watts

'Addlestone's latest Service victim is Corpl. W. J. Watts, of the Royal Engineers, whose father lives at 29, Chapel Avenue.

The deceased, a bricklayer by occupation and 30 years of age, joined H. M. Forces the month war was declared, and eleven months ago went across to France. Three weeks ago he was invalided back to England, suffering from asphyxiating gas and appendicitis. Corpl. Watts was taken to the Epsom Military Hospital, where he passed away on Tuesday.

Arrangements have been made to give deceased a military funeral, and the body will be interred at the Addlestone cemetery on Tuesday afternoon next, at 3 o'clock.

Mr. Watts has another son serving in the Canadian Artillery.' (The Surrey Herald, May 12, 1916)

'A military funeral took place on Tuesday, at Addlestone cemetery, when the remains of the late Corpl. Watts, Royal Engineers, whose father lives at 29, Chapel Avenue, Addlestone, and whose death from appendicitis and asphyxiating gas we reported last week, were interred with full military honours.

The coffin was borne on a gun-carriage, and was enveloped by a Union Jack. A section of the Royal Engineers from Burvale (Hersham) was present at the church and the graveside, and as a last tribute to the fallen hero fired three volleys over the grave, whilst two buglers sounded the Last Post. The hat which deceased wore at the Battle of Loos, when it was penetrated by a bullet, was also placed on the coffin. Among the mourners were: Mr. and Mrs. Watts (father and mother), Mr. and Mrs. Mitchell (sister and brother-in-law), Mr. and Mrs. Puckeridge (sister and brother-in-law), Mr. James Watts (brother) and the Misses Annie, Alice, Nellie, Ethel and Dorothy Watts (sisters). Numerous friends followed to the church and were present at the graveside. The service was conducted by the Rev. Pickering, and Mr. D. Steer was the undertaker.

Floral tributes were received from: Mother and Dad; Hetty and Stan; brother Jim; Lizzie and George; Annie, Alice, Nelly, Ethel and Dorry; Albert and Nellie (Canada); aunt and uncle; George and Edie; Mrs. Gosden; Maggie and Daisy; Mrs. Bailey and family; Mr. H. Lee; a comrade's family; Chapel Park School; Mr. and Mrs. Macey; Harry Basson; an old pal; Bill's pals; Aunt Sallie and cousins; Mr. and Mrs. H. Gosden; Mr. and Mrs. Barnes and family; Mrs. J.S.; a mother of five soldiers; S. Gosden; members of National Reserve Club; Mr. and Mrs. E. Lovelock; Mrs. Lovelock and Mrs. Goodman; Sergt. A. Agatter and Cpl. F. O'Farrell, Ottermead Hospital – two comrades.

Mr. and Mrs. Watts and family wish to thank the numerous friends for their kind messages and for the beautiful wreaths sent on the death of their eldest son.' (The Surrey Herald, May 19, 1916)

WEEDING, John Richard Baggallay

Second Lieutenant, 2nd Bn. Welsh Regiment
Born in Addlestone, 21 March 1882
Son of Thomas W. Weeding (d.1929) and Alice Maude Elizabeth Weeding, née Brinkley (d.1926), of Kingthorpe, Addlestone (m.1876)
Killed in action, 22 December 1914, near Festubert, France, age 32
Awards: MENTIONED IN DESPATCHES
Cemetery: BROWN'S ROAD MILITARY CEMETERY, FESTUBERT, Pas de Calais, France
Memorial window: St Paul's, Addlestone, destroyed by fire in 2003 and not included in the restoration

'Mr. and Mrs. T. W. Weeding, of Addlestone, have received a communication from the Officer Commanding the Welsh Regiment in Flanders, which states that he believes that Second-Lieutenant J. R. B. Weeding, their younger son, has been killed. It was explained that after an attack on German trenches near Ypres, led by a senior lieutenant and Lieut. Weeding, the senior was wounded, and the latter was believed to have been killed. Mrs. Weeding still entertains the hope that her son is alive and in the absence of further official news her hopes appear to be justified.

Mr. Richard Weeding, as he was best known, was a son of Mr. T. W. Weeding (Clerk of the Peace and Clerk to the Surrey County Council), and of Mrs. Weeding, and before the war was a member of the staff at the County Hall, Kingston. He was at the front attached to the Welsh Regiment. Just before the war started he resigned his appointment at Kingston, and went to Shanghai. At the time of his departure the Surrey County Council recorded their appreciation of his services and their regret at losing him. When war broke out he, putting aside all private considerations, returned and enlisted in the Royal Flying Corps, and went on active service almost immediately. Subsequently he was given a commission in the Welsh Regiment.

It is to be sincerely hoped that Mrs. Weeding's hopes will be realised, for the Lieutenant was very popular. Of commanding physique, he was once captain of the Marlborough Nomads F.C., and had a fine athletic career. His age is thirty-two.

Captain Weeding, the other son of Mr. and Mrs. Weeding, who was wounded by shrapnel in October, is making slow progress towards recovery.' (The Surrey Herald, January 8, 1915)

'It is being presumed that Second-Lieut. J. R. B. Weeding has been killed in action (as reported in our last issue). The Surrey County Council at its meeting on Tuesday passed a vote of sympathy with its Clerk (Mr. T. W. Weeding, J.P.) and with Mrs. Weeding in the loss of their younger son. This was moved by the Chairman, and seconded by the Vice-Chairman, who expressed the Council's admiration at the manner of the Lieutenant's death, and referred to the excellent service given to the Council by him during the eight years he had been employed at the County Hall. His action in giving up his private affairs and joining the Army, it was said, would be cherished as an example to all young Englishmen.' (The Surrey Herald, January 15, 1915)

'All doubts as to the fate of Lieut. J. R. B. Weeding, of the 2nd Welsh Regt., (the second son of Mr. and Mrs. T. W. Weeding, of Kingthorpe, Addlestone), have been dispelled by the discovery of his body by brother officers.

It was on Dec. 22nd that Lieut. Weeding, who joined the Services on the outbreak of war, accompanied by a couple of score or so of men attacked the German trenches at Festubert, near La Bassee. Some of the men returned, but not so Lieut. Weeding – and none of his friends would have expected him to do that unless his mission had been fully accomplished. The following day a brother officer thought he recognised Lieut. Weeding's body lying between the British and German trenches – the Addlestonian was wearing a Burberry, and his huge frame assisted in the identification. There was no indication of life, and consequently no incentive to endeavour to render aid in the bullet and shrapnel swept territory either by day or night. Curiously enough, the officer was wearing Lieut. Weeding's second coat when he considered he established the identification.

There, with shells and bullets passing over it by the thousand, the body was lying for several weeks until the recent British advance, when it was recognised by some officers of the Gloucester Regt. and given a British soldier's burial on the battlefield. A cigarette case, a £5 note, and other things found in the deceased officer's haversack have been returned to the parents.' (The Surrey Herald, March 19, 1915)

WEEDING, Thomas

Major, 1st Bn. Queen's (Royal West Surrey Regiment)
Born in Addlestone, 7 July 1879
Son of Thomas W. Weeding (d.1929) and Alice Maude Elizabeth
Weeding, née Brinkley (d.1926) of Kingthorpe, Addlestone (m.1876)
Killed in action, 26 August 1917, near Koksijde, West-Vlaanderen,
Belgium, age 38
Cemetery: COXYDE MILITARY CEMETERY, Koksijde, West-
Vlaanderen, Belgium
Memorial window: St Paul's, Addlestone, destroyed by fire in 2003 and
not included in the restoration

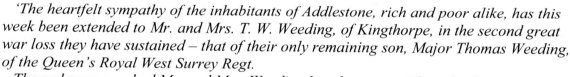

'The heartfelt sympathy of the inhabitants of Addlestone, rich and poor alike, has this week been extended to Mr. and Mrs. T. W. Weeding, of Kingthorpe, in the second great war loss they have sustained – that of their only remaining son, Major Thomas Weeding, of the Queen's Royal West Surrey Regt.

The sad news reached Mr. and Mrs. Weeding by telegram on Thursday last, to be quickly followed by the sympathetic letters appended. Our readers scarcely need reminding that the younger son, Sec.-Lieut. J. R. B. Weeding, of the Welsh Regt., was killed on Dec. 22nd, 1914.

MAJOR WEEDING'S CAREER.

Born in 1879, the late Major T. Weeding was educated at Marlborough College and passed through Sandhurst, being gazetted to the 1st Battalion of the Queen's, then in India, where he spent eight years. He was a keen polo player, and a very good shot. He was among the first 100 officers to learn to fly, but had to rejoin his regiment in Bermuda before the R.F.C. was formed. He came back from South Africa with the Queen's at the beginning of the war, and went through all the heavy fighting near Ypres in October, 1914, being wounded on the 31st. He was again wounded on September 30, 1915, so seriously that he was unable to go out again till December, 1916. On August 26, as he was riding up to the front, a shell burst near him and he and his horse were killed instantaneously.

TESTIMONY TO HIS QUALITIES.

Lieut.-Col. L. M. Crofts, Commanding the Battalion, has written:- "It is with the greatest pain and sorrow I have to write and tell you that your son was killed this morning. He was riding up to look at the front line trenches, together with three other officers, but when he had got about half way there and was still some two miles from the trenches, the Germans started shelling a Battery near the road, and one shell struck the road close to them. Major Weeding and his horse were killed instantaneously, and two of the other three officers were wounded. His body has been brought back to this village and will be buried in the military cemetery with military honours. There is traffic going up this road all day and it was sheer bad luck that the party should have just run into this burst of shell fire. I have known your son for a long time and served with him for a great part of the war, and a braver or more gallant officer I have never met."

The following letter has reached Mr. Weeding from Brig.-General Baird:- "I write to express to you and Mrs. Weeding my great sorrow at the loss of your son and offer you my deepest sympathy in your great sadness. It is many months now since your son came back to the old Battalion, at a time when he was badly needed; and since he came I can only say that no officer has ever worked harder or more successfully at his duties. His loss is indeed a sad one for us all – the Battalion, the Brigade, and most of all, as I feel only too surely, to you and Mrs. Weeding. Nothing I can say can, I know, do much to comfort you in your great sorrow, but I hope it may help you to bear up to know how much he was looked up to and admired by all his comrades in the Brigade. The funeral took place this morning, and I am glad to say that circumstances made it possible for it to be carried out as he would have wished it to be – in the presence of his own gallant men and with representatives from all the units who had come to show their sympathy with them in their own sorrow for the loss of a gallant comrade." (The Surrey Herald, September 7, 1917)

WELLS, Frederick Thomas

Private 365108, 1/7th (City of London) Bn. London Regiment
Born in Lewes, Sussex, 1899
Son of William Edwin and Annie Wells, née Turner, of Station Road,
Addlestone (1911 census) (m.1889)
Killed in action, 3 July 1918, France, age 18
Cemetery: CONTAY BRITISH CEMETERY, CONTAY, Somme,
France

'The sad news reached Mr. and Mrs. E. W. Wells, Station-road, on Monday evening that their son, Pte. Fredk. T. Wells, the London Regt., had been killed in France on July 2nd.

The young soldier would not have attained his 19th birthday until next Saturday. He joined the Forces last November, prior to which he had been a Cadet in the local Volunteer Co. His parents never had the satisfaction of seeing their boy in khaki, as he crossed to France without having any home leave from the day he went to Guildford Barracks for his medical examination.

The news was conveyed by a letter from a chum, Pte. N. Barnes, who wrote that Pte. Wells was killed by a shell at 10.30 on July 2nd. He was carried down to the aid post, but passed away, just as he arrived there. The writer forwarded some photos he found in Pte. Wells' pack, adding that his other belongings would be sent in due course by the War Office.

Mr. and Mrs. Wells and family wish to thank the numerous persons who have expressed sympathy with them in their great loss.' (The Surrey Herald, July 12, 1918)

'THE LATE PTE. F. T. WELLS, whose death was recorded in our last issue, would not have attained his 19th birthday until next September. Mr. and Mrs. E. W. Wells' elder son is serving in the R.A.M.C. at Salonica. He enlisted in January, 1915, and has not been home for over three years.' (The Surrey Herald, July 19, 1918)

WHEELER, Henry Harold

Rifleman R/41256, 2/15th (County of London) Bn. London Regiment (Prince of Wales's Own Civil Service Rifles). Formerly King's Royal Rifle Corps
Born in Reading, 23 October 1898
Son of Henry and Alice Wheeler, née Mayo, of Common Lane, New Haw, Addlestone (Register of Electors 1918) (m.1892)
Killed in action, 27 July 1918, Belgium, age 19
Cemetery: KLEIN-VIERSTRAAT BRITISH CEMETERY, Heuvelland, West-Vlaanderen, Belgium

'IN MEMORIAM.

WHEELER – In loving memory of our beloved son, Rfm. Henry H. Wheeler, King's Royal Rifles, who was killed in action, 27th July, 1918. Mourned by his sorrowing Parents, Sisters, Brothers and Friends.' (The Surrey Herald, August 1, 1919)

WHITE, Charles Philip

Private 6130, 1st Bn. East Surrey Regiment
Born in Addlestone, 1881
Son of Henry Thomas and Eliza White, of Station Road, Addlestone (1891 census); husband of Alice White, née Voice, of Chapel Park Road, Addlestone (1911 census) (m.1910)
Killed in action, 28 October 1914, in trenches north of La Bassée, France, age 33
Cemetery: PONT-DU-HEM MILITARY CEMETERY, LA GORGUE, Nord, France

'Mystery still surrounds the wellbeing of Pte. C. White, 1st East Surrey Regiment, of Chapel Park, who was called up on the Reserve at the commencement of the war. An official communication was received on October 26th, by Mrs. White, stating that her husband was posted as missing since October 10th, whilst she received a note direct from him under date October 26th, saying he was all right and cheerful, but having a rough time. Other intimations were received from the War Office, one on November 26th, stating that White was wounded, and still later, on December 3rd, another stated that he had been killed in action. Pte. White was formerly a labourer employed by Messrs. Tarrants, and latterly he had been groundsman at the Tennis Courts, St. George's Hills. He had been twelve years in the Army and had re-signed on the reserve for an extended period.

Mrs. White is left with two small children, their ages being three years and eighteen months.' (The Surrey Herald, December 11, 1914)

'Definite news of Pte. C. White, whose home is at 5, Thomas Cottages, Chapel Park Road, is apparently not yet forthcoming.

Pte. White, who was in the 1st East Surrey Regiment, served eight years in the Regular Army and subsequently four years in the Reserve. He was called up for service on August 5th last year. Letters were received by his wife dated up to October 26th on which date he seemed to be quite all right. Before his last letter was received, however, Mrs. White heard from the War Office saying he was reported missing. Another report arrived on Nov. 24th stating that he was wounded, whilst on Dec. 3rd an official intimation was received that he was killed on Oct. 28th. Nothing further was heard until Sunday, when his regimental number, together with a purse supposed to have been found on his body, was received from the War Office. None of the articles known to have been in his possession were, however, included.

Pte. White has a cousin, Corpl. J. White, in the same battalion of the East Surreys, and it is a strange coincidence that the purse should contain his photograph. Mrs. White believes that a mistake has been made and that her husband is a prisoner of war in Germany.' (The Surrey Herald, March 5, 1915)

WHITE, James
Private 9296, 1st Bn. East Surrey Regiment
Born in Chelmsford, 1891
Son of Robert and Margaret White, née Collins (d.1898) of Conquest Road, Addlestone (1911 census) (m.1879)
Killed in action, 23 November 1914, in trenches east of Lindenhoek, Belgium, age 23
Memorial: YPRES (MENIN GATE) MEMORIAL, Ieper, West-Vlaanderen, Belgium

WOODGER, Walter Thomas Stanley
Company Sergeant Major 44208, 62nd Field Coy., Royal Engineers
Born in Addlestone, 11 August 1890
Son of Walter and Esther Emily Woodger, née Cartwright (m.1882), of Rosebery Villa, Addlestone
Killed in action, 21 March 1918, near St Quentin, France, age 27
Awards: MILITARY MEDAL
Cemetery: GRAND-SERAUCOURT BRITISH CEMETERY, Aisne, France

'Sergt. W. T. Woodger has been awarded the Military Medal for distinguished conduct and special devotion to duty. The Sergeant joined the Forces on the outbreak of war, and has served 15 months in France with a Field Company of the Corps of Royal Engineers, attached to a famous Scottish Division, which has taken part in some of the most important actions on the Western Front. He was recently reported slightly wounded, but has sufficiently recovered to be back again with his unit.

Sergt. Woodger is the son of Mr. W. Woodger, the well-known local tradesman.' (The Surrey Herald, October 27, 1916)

'Joining up in August, 1914, the late Co. Sergt.-Major W. T. S. Woodger, Royal Engineers – whose death was recorded in our last issue – very soon made himself popular with his officers and comrades, and by strict attention and energies quickly won his stripes, so that on crossing to France, attached to a famous Scottish Division, he went as Sergeant. During the ups and downs of the 1915 – 16 – 17 campaigns, Sergt. Woodger saw much fighting, and was twice wounded. October 19, 1916, saw him decorated on the field with the Military Medal by the General of the Division, and 1917 saw him still further promoted to Company Sergeant-Major.

From a communication received by his parents, from the Lieutenant of the Company, it would appear that the Sergt.-Major and Lieutenant were engaged running from dug-out to dug-out on March 21st, in an endeavour to save the lives of their men as much as possible, when a shell burst nearly over the two officers, the Sergt.-Major being almost instantly killed.

The Commanding Officer, officers and men have conveyed their sympathy to the family, and expressed their sorrow at losing so good a man and comrade.' (The Surrey Herald, April 19, 1918)

'*SERGEANT WOODGER'S LETTER*

Dear Vicar,

It is a little over three months since I left England for France, but to me it seems a much longer time and the new experiences and awful work which I and my comrades have had to face would fill many chapters of a book. But I often think the anxiety and suspense is much greater for those at home than it is for us out here. No doubt you in England have had good cause to rejoice when reading the recent accounts of the great victories which have been achieved on our side. To us who participated in those great battles of September 25th and 26th, with all the magnificence of victory, it was simply awful. When looking back, one wonders how ever a single man came out of those most terrible engagements alive.

One little incident I remember, was when we were ordered to hold the first and second line of German trenches at all costs. Standing there, as it were face to face with death, with the dead bodies of many brave men around us, a fellow close by me remarked "Ah! They're just coming out of Church now." It was Sunday night, and I could not help wondering if they had realized what was going on in this terrible country. Even a little incident like this will turn one's thoughts to home and make a man realize what he is really fighting for.' (Addlestone Parish Magazine, November 1915)

APPENDIX 1

SOME OTHERS WITH CONNECTIONS IN THE ADDLESTONE AREA WHO GAVE THEIR LIVES IN THE GREAT WAR AND WHOSE NAMES ARE NOT INSCRIBED ON THE VICTORY PARK MEMORIAL GATES

BAILEY, Frank Willson

Corporal 67674, 136th Army Troops Coy., Royal Engineers
Born in Boxmoor, Herts., 1879
Baptised, 26 January 1879, Hemel Hempstead
Son of Thomas Willson and Emma Bailey, née Fretten, of Watford (1891 census);
husband of Francis Mary Bailey, née Clark, of Chapel Grove, Addlestone (m.1910)
Died, 20 September 1915, Lemnos, during the Gallipoli campaign, age 36
Cemetery: PORTIANOS MILITARY CEMETERY, Lemnos, Greece

BALCHIN, Edward

Lance Corporal 22546, 1st Garrison Battalion, Essex Regiment
Born in Addlestone, 1880
Son of William (d.1897) and Elizabeth Balchin, née Longhurst, of
Station Road, Chertsey
Died, 31 October 1915, in Chichester, age 36
Cemetery: CHICHESTER CEMETERY, Sussex, United Kingdom

*'The war has claimed another Addlestone victim, this time in Corpl.
Edward Balchin. Corpl. Balchin, who lived with his brother at Ivy
Cottage, Simplemarsh Lane, joined the Royal Sussex Regiment on the
outbreak of war, but was later transferred to another Regiment. He contracted dysentery
in Egypt, and passed away in a Chichester Hospital on Sunday. The deceased N.C.O. was
38 years of age.' (The Surrey Herald, November 5, 1915)*

BREWER, Frederick James

Leading Seaman 210226, H.M.S. *Warspite*
Enlisted, 20 October 1902
Born in Brixton, London, 20 October 1884
Son of Frederick (deceased) and Sarah E. Brewer, of Conquest Road, Addlestone
Died, 7 May 1915, on H.M. Hospital Ship *Plassy*, from a fractured base of skull, age 30

H.M.S. *Warspite*, a Dreadnought battleship of 27,500 tons was launched in 1913. She
took part in the Battle of Jutland on 31 May 1916 and saw action throughout the Second
World War. She was broken up in 1947.

H.M.H.S. *Plassy,* 7,400 tons, was launched in 1900 as a passenger ship. She was
converted to a hospital ship and based at Scapa Flow in the Great War. She was broken
up in 1924.
Cemetery: OSMONDWALL CEMETERY, Hoy, Orkney Islands, United Kingdom

BRUNNING, Henry

Gunner 205077, 218th Siege Bty. Royal Garrison Artillery
Born in Winston, Suffolk, 1881
Son of Abraham and Kesiah Brunning of Winston, Suffolk (1891 census); husband of Ellen Brunning, née Mason (m.1905) (d.1907); father of Dorothy Ellen Brunning, of Spinney Hill, Addlestone (b.1907)
Died of wounds, 25 September 1918, No. 55 Casualty Clearing Station, Doingt, France, age 37
Cemetery: DOINGT COMMUNAL CEMETERY EXTENSION, Somme, France

BUTLER, Arthur

Private 47275, 2nd Bn. Lancashire Fusiliers
Formerly 241473, Middlesex Regiment
Born in Hackney, 1896
Son of Frederick Alfred and Emma Butler, née Hulton, of Brighton Road, Addlestone (m.1880)
Died of wounds, 30 October 1918, age 23
Cemetery: NEW SOUTHGATE CEMETERY, Hertfordshire, United Kingdom

CAMPBELL, Quentin Hewes

Captain, 1/5th Bn. King's Own (Yorkshire Light Infantry)
Born in Lanarkshire, Scotland, c1894
Son of Quentin and Annie Campbell, of Old Monkland, Lanarkshire (1901 census); husband of Eleanor Kathleen Campbell, née Lightburne, of Hillfield, Station Road, Addlestone (m.1915). Father of Catherine M. Campbell (b.1917)
Killed in action, 19 July 1917, age 23
Cemetery: RAMSCAPPELLE ROAD MILITARY CEMETERY, Belgium

'We have to chronicle with deep regret the death, in action in France, of Capt. Quentin Hewes Campbell, of the King's Own Yorkshire Light Infantry, whose wife resides at Hillfield, Station Road, Addlestone.

The first news of the Captain's death arrived early in the week, by an official telegram, which stated that the deceased fell whilst leading an attack on the 19th inst. In addition to the War Office notification, letters have been received from the General Commanding the Division, also from the Major-General and the Captain-Adjutant.

General Moxon has written as follows: "You will have heard of the sad death of your gallant husband, and I can assure you that it is most distressing to me to offer you my sincerest expressions of deepest sympathy. When your husband met his end, he was leading a party in daylight to surprise and capture an enemy post. It was an enterprise which he suggested himself, and which I approved. The audacity and expeditiousness of the operation proved successful, but unfortunately your courageous husband outstripped his escort, and though he was seen to shoot two of the enemy, he was killed before the post could be finally rushed. I am glad to say his splendid death was well revenged, but nothing can restore to me his fearless and sound leadership. In your deplorable bereavement I am sure you will be proud of the thought that your gallant husband had endeared himself to everyone, and that his officers and men had unbounded confidence in his ability, and would have followed him everywhere. Some of his Company went through *a severe enemy barrage to recover his body, and after some time succeeded, and he will be given a Christian burial."*

The Major-General, in the course of a very sympathetic letter to the widow, says: "He was a very gallant officer, and a fine leader of men, and had frequently displayed great courage and ability under very trying circumstances."

The late Capt. Campbell was only 23 years of age. On the outbreak of war he enlisted as a private in the 4th City of London Regt. After serving 11 months in Malta he was gazetted as a Second Lieutenant in the K.O.Y.L.I. (Territorial Battn.). He crossed to France in September, 1916. and a few months later gained his Captaincy and also the Military Cross for exceptional gallantry in the field.' (The Surrey Herald, July 27, 1917)

CHANNELL, Frederick Edmund

Private 187, 3rd Bn. Queen's (Royal West Surrey Regiment)
Born in Long Ditton, 2 November 1876
Son of William and Sarah Channell (d.1902), of Chapel Grove, Addlestone (1901 census); husband of Margaret Amy Channell, née Kenneison, of West Street, Woking (m.1903)
Died, 7 October 1917, age 40
Cemetery: BROOKWOOD CEMETERY, Woking, United Kingdom

COUSINS, Arthur Frederick

Corporal G/7555, 11th Bn. Queen's (Royal West Surrey Regiment)
Born in Sunningdale, 1889
Son of Henry Joseph and Emily Anne Cousins, née Gambriel, (d.1909); foster son of Mrs M. Stacey, of Charlotte Villas, Addlestone Moor
Died of wounds, 4 October 1918, age 29
Cemetery: LIJSSENTHOEK MILITARY CEMETERY, Poperinge, West-Vlaanderen, Belgium

CRABB, Norman Frederick

Private 307514, 561723, Prince of Wales's Own (West Yorkshire Regiment)
Born in Addlestone, 1897
Son of Rufus and Fanny Maria Crabb, née Brewer, of Addlestone Hill (1911 census); husband of Kate Crabb, née Slemmings (m.1926)
Died, 14 September 1936, from the effects of mustard gas poisoning sustained in Belgium in 1917, age 39
Cemetery: CHERTSEY, Surrey, United Kingdom

'RIFLM. NORMAN CRABB, youngest son of Mr. and Mrs. R. Crabb, of Addlestone Hill, has been home on sick leave, after being seriously gassed at Nieuport on the 22nd July. He joined H.M. Forces in May, 1916, and crossed to France the beginning of November. Now he has gone to Ripon for convalescence.' (The Surrey Herald, November 2, 1917)

'19 YEARS AFTER
Mr. NORMAN F. CRABB SUCCUMBS TO MUSTARD GAS.

The interment took place in Chertsey cemetery last Thursday of Mr. Norman Frederick Crabb, whose death at the early age of 39 occurred at his parents' home, 114 Chertsey Road, Addlestone, on the previous Monday. During the war he served with the West Yorks

Regiment, and was badly gassed at Nieuport, Belgium, in 1917. After years of suffering he gradually became worse, until mustard gas claimed another victim.

The chief mourners were: The widow, Messrs. Rufus, Arthur and Reginald Crabb (brothers), Mr. R. Bassett (brother-in-law), Mrs. A. Crabb (sister-in-law), Mr. Slemmings (father-in-law), Mr. and Mrs. Gosden (brother-in-law and sister-in-law).' (The Surrey Herald, September 18, 1936)

EXCELL, Harry
Private TF/241501, 1/8th Bn. Duke of Cambridge's Own (Middlesex Regiment)
Born in Remenham, Berkshire, 1885
Son of Ephraim and Ellen Excell, née Ind (d.1890) of Clermount, New Haw Road, Addlestone (1924 Register of Electors)
Killed in action, 16 August 1917, during the Battle of Langemarck, part of the Third Battle of Ypres (Passchendaele), age 32
Memorial: TYNE COT MEMORIAL, Zonnebeke, West-Vlaanderen, Belgium

EYLES, Bertram Alfred
Private PO/16333, Royal Marine Light Infantry
Born in Folksworth, Huntingdonshire, 1894
Son of Joseph (d.1920) and Jane Elizabeth Eyles, née Mitchell, of "Bournville", Crockford Park Road, Addlestone (m.1877)
Killed in action, 31 May 1916, on H.M.S. *Black Prince*, age 22
Memorial: PORTSMOUTH NAVAL MEMORIAL, Hampshire, United Kingdom

H.M.S. *Black Prince*, commissioned in 1906, was an armoured cruiser of 13,550 tons. She was sunk during the night of 31 May/1 June 1916 during the Battle of Jutland while separated from the British fleet. Gunfire from a line of German warships resulted in the *Black Prince* blowing up with the loss of all her crew of 862 men.

EYLES, Thomas Frederick
Private 104352, 123rd Bn. Machine Gun Corps (Infantry)
Born in Washingley, Huntingdonshire, 1898
Son of Joseph (d.1920) and Jane Elizabeth Eyles, née Mitchell, of "Bournville", Crockford Park Road, Addlestone (m.1877)
Killed in action, 26 September 1917, Belgium, age 19
Cemetery: HOOGE CRATER CEMETERY, Ieper, West-Vlaanderen, Belgium

FESTING, Arthur Hoskyns
Major, 1st Bn. Royal Irish Rifles
Born in Maiden Bradley, Wiltshire, 9 February 1869
Son of Henry Blathwayt Festing (d.1900) and Mary Eliza Festing, née Todd (d.1908), of Bois Hall, Addlestone. Served in the South African War (1899-1900) and in earlier African campaigns
Killed in action, 9 May 1917, during the Battle of Aubers, age 45
Awards: Companion of the Order of St Michael and St George (1902); Distinguished Service Order (1899)
Memorial: PLOEGSTEERT MEMORIAL, Comines-Warneton, Hainaut, Belgium

FLINT, Sidney Edwin
Private 229280, Royal Canadian Regiment
Born in Addlestone, 15 November 1880
Embarked, Liverpool, 1 November 1906, on SS *Ionian*, for Montreal, Canada
Son of George Thomas Flint, Railway Station Master at Addlestone (d.1902), and Sarah Ann Flint, née Blackmore (d.1890)
Died, 3 November 1916, France, during the Battle of the Somme, age 35
Cemetery: PORTE-DE-PARIS CEMETERY, CAMBRAI, Nord, France

GARLAND, John

Private 9932, 8th Bn. East Surrey Regiment
Born in Ottershaw, 1891
Son of George and Jane Garland, of Rose Cottage, Brox Road, Ottershaw (m. 1887)
Died of wounds, 6 July 1916, sustained during the Battle of the Somme, age 25.
Cemetery: ST. SEVER CEMETERY, ROUEN, France

'Information has reached Mrs. Garland, of Rose Cottage, Brox–road, that her son, Pte. John Garland, of the 7th Battn. East Surrey Regt., was wounded last week in France.

Pte. J. Garland, who is 25 years of age, previously to enlisting was employed locally as a gardener. He enlisted in July, 1915, and crossed to France at the beginning of December.

Buried by a shell, Pte Garland appears to have been wounded three times in the left leg and twice in the right arm, though apparently the wounds are not very serious. He is now in a Winchester Hospital, making satisfactory progress.' (The Surrey Herald, March 17. 1916)

'Reference was made in a recent issue to the fact that Pte. J. Garland, of the East Surreys – whose mother resides in Brox-road, Ottershaw – had been seriously wounded and was lying in a hospital at Rouen. On Wednesday morning of this week Mrs. Garland received information that her son had succumbed to his wounds.' (The Surrey Herald, July 14, 1916)

GENTLE, Francis (Frank) George

Sergeant 8502, 7th Bn. Prince of Wales's (North Staffordshire Regiment)
Born in Putney, 2 October 1889
Son of Louisa Eleanor Gentle, (d.1912); husband of Elizabeth Amelia Gentle, née Hyde (m.1914); son-in-law of Benjamin and Caroline Hyde, of the Gardener's Arms, Ottershaw (1911 census)
Killed in action, 8 August 1915, during the Battle of Sari Bair, part of the Gallipoli campaign, age 25
Cemetery: 7th FIELD AMBULANCE CEMETERY, Turkey

'It is with the deepest regret that we have to record the news of the death of Col.-Sergt.-Major Gentle of the 7th Batt. North Staffordshire Regt., who was killed whilst attacking the Turks in the Dardanelles on August 8th. The deceased N.C.O. was the son-in-law of Mr. and Mrs. Hyde, of the Gardeners Arms, having married their eldest daughter in July, 1914.

Col.-Sergt.-Major Gentle returned home on leave from India about six months previously to the breaking out of hostilities, being then attached to the 2nd Batt. of the North Staffordshire Regt., which is still in India. For several months, he was stationed at Blackdown Camp, engaged in training Lord Kitchener's Army.

The sad news reached his wife on Tuesday morning, being conveyed to her by a Sergt. of the same company. The following are extracts from the letter:

"It is with the profoundest regret that I write to tell you that your husband was killed in action on August 8th, whilst attacking the enemy. His Company was put to a rather hard task, having to charge the enemy up a steep hill, where several met their fate. His death was instantaneous, as he was riddled with bullets from a machine gun. He was a good soldier, and he will be missed by his Company and Co. Officers, whilst the deeds done by his Company that day will not readily be forgotten. Please accept our heartfelt sympathy." (The Surrey Herald, September 3, 1915)

HAMPTON, Arthur

Private 1044, 46th Bn. Australian Infantry, Australian Imperial Force
Enlisted, 9 March 1915
Born in Bramley, Surrey, 1891
Embarked, Tilbury, 9 July 1914, on HMAT *Port Lincoln*, for Melbourne
Son of Henry and Harriet Hampton, née Garrett of Victoria Road, Addlestone (1911 census) (m.1873)
Killed in action, 5 April 1918, France, during the Battle of the Ancre, age 27
Cemetery: MILLENCOURT COMMUNAL CEMETERY EXTENSION, Somme, France

'Pte. A. Hampton, of the Australian Expeditionary Force, the youngest son of Mr. and Mrs. H. Hampton, of Victoria Road, has been killed in France. Mrs. Hampton has received a letter from the Colonel, in which he says that Pte. Hampton was killed instantly by a shell. Pte. Hampton emigrated to Australia four years ago, and joined up on the outbreak of war. He has since served in Egypt, Gallipoli and France. Mrs. Hampton has another son, a prisoner-of-war in Germany.' (The Surrey Herald, April 19, 1918)

HARDS, Frederick

Sapper 550646, 517th Field Coy., Corps of Royal Engineers
Born in Battersea, 1890
Son of Stephen and Lucy Hards, of Battersea (1891 census); husband of Lilian Elizabeth Aird, formerly Hards, née Deeks, m.1915, of Ecton Road, Addlestone
Died of wounds, 4 June 1917, at 17th Casualty Clearing Station, Remy, Pas de Calais, France, age 27
Cemetery: LIJSSENTHOEK MILITARY CEMETERY, Poperinge, West-Vlaanderen, Belgium

'We regret we have to record to-day the death in France of yet another Addlestone soldier, in the person of Sapper Frederick Hards, of the Royal Engineers, whose wife resides at 16, Ecton-road, and formerly at Station-road, West Byfleet.

The sad intimation was received by the widow during last week-end, in the form of an official telegram, Chaplain's letter, and a letter from the deceased's comrade. The following are extracts from the comrade's letter:- "This is to inform you that your husband, Sapper F. Hards, has been wounded and has since died of the effects of his wounds and gas, which entered his system. It happened in this way. We had finished our job for the night, and as there were two lorries going our way back we jumped into one and had done about two miles when the enemy put up a barrage of gas and shells just in front of us. The driver pulled up, and we thought of making a run for our lives across the fields, but as we were getting out the motor started off again and we had to remain where we were, with the result that a shell dropped under the back of the lorry, wounding Fred and gassing the driver of the A.S.C. I myself had a narrow escape. Fred then said he was wounded in the stomach. He was wounded at 2 a.m. on the 3rd, and died on the 4th inst."

The Chaplain's letter, which was despatched from the 17th Casualty Clearing Station, showed that Sapper Hards had died at 4.30 a.m. on the 4th inst. He entered the Station a few hours earlier, badly wounded in the chest and also been gassed. The letter stated that there was no hope from the first. His body was interred in the Military Cemetery at Remey, two miles S.W. of Poyeringhe.

The late Sapper Hards, who was 27 years of age, had been in France for 17 months, and unfortunately did not have the opportunity of seeing his home once during that period. He joined the Forces in June, 1915. Prior to enlisting the deceased was employed as a carpenter and joiner at Battersea.' (The Surrey Herald, June 15, 1917)

HARMS, Arthur
Lance Corporal 204885, 2nd Bn. Devonshire Regiment
Born in Guildford, 1879
Son of Alfred (d.1889) and Elizabeth Harms, née Dawes, of Caversham Road, Reading, (m.1870); previously of Lime Villa, Addlestone (1881 census)
Killed in action, 29 November 1917, Belgium, age 38
Memorial: TYNE COT MEMORIAL, Zonnebeke, West-Vlaanderen, Belgium

'In France the death recently occurred of Lce.-Corpl. Arthur Harms, The Devons, age 38. The deceased was the son of the late Mr. Alfred Harms, of Addlestone, and Mrs. A. Harms, now residing at De Montford-road, Reading.' (The Surrey Herald, January 18, 1918)

HARRIS, Thomas
Private G/13531, 1st Bn. Queen's (Royal West Surrey Regiment)
Born in Addlestone, 1887
Son of Charles Henry and Ann Harris, née Stevens, of Addlestone (m.1873); husband of Elizabeth Warren (formerly Harris, née Lemon, m.1915) of Birchwood Road, West Byfleet
Died of wounds, 12 April 1918, age 31
Cemetery: LIJSSENTHOEK MILITARY CEMETERY, Poperinge, West-Vlaanderen, Belgium

HAZELL, William John
Private McG/201, Princess Patricia's Canadian Light Infantry (Eastern Ontario Regiment)
Enlisted, 15 June 1915, Montreal, Canada
Born in Chertsey, 28 March 1887
Baptised, 15 May 1887, St Peter's, Chertsey
Embarked, Bristol, 15 May 1912, on SS *Royal George*, for Montreal, Canada
Son of William John (d.1895) and Annie Louisa Hazell, née Kynaston, of The White Hart, New Haw (1892-1905); husband of Harriett Adelaide Jessie Hazell, née

Collembeck, (m.26 November 1913, at Calvary Congregational Church, Montreal); father of Marjorie Louisa Hazell (b.17 October 1914 in Montreal; baptised, 11 November 1914 at Calvary Congregational Church, Montreal)
Killed in action, 2 June 1916, during a German attack on Canadian positions at Sanctuary Wood, Flanders, age 29
Memorial: YPRES (MENIN GATE) MEMORIAL, Ieper, West-Vlaanderen, Belgium

HEADEACH, Maurice Charles Pilford

Sergeant 12/392, 12th (Service) (Sheffield) Bn. York and Lancaster Regiment
Born in Todmorden, Lancashire, 12 January 1874
Son of The Rev. Albert Workman Headeach (1840-1937) and Alice Jane Headeach, née Wraith, (m.1869) of Addlestone; husband of Charlotte Jemima Headeach, née Cruikshank of Bangalore House, Stokenchurch, Bucks (m.1914); brother of The Rev. Arnold Hope Wraith Headeach (1878-1978), curate at St Paul's, Addlestone (1912-1917)
Killed in action, 1 July 1916, France, the first day of the Battle of the Somme, during the attack towards Serre, age 42
Awards: MILITARY MEDAL
Cemetery: RAILWAY HOLLOW CEMETERY, HEBUTERNE, Pas de Calais, France
Memorial window: St Peter & Paul, Stokenchurch

HILL, Alfred (served as SMITH)

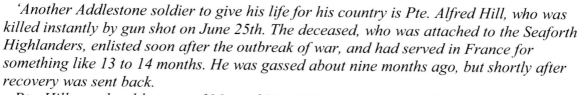

Private S/7436, 2nd Bn. Seaforth Highlanders
Born in Guildford, 1887
Son of John and Rosah Ellen Hill, née Lampard, of Sheath Cottage, Thames Ditton (m.1876); formerly of Common Lane, New Haw (1911 census)
Killed in action, 25 June 1916, France, near Mailly-Maillet, when his battalion came under bombardment from German artillery, age 28
Cemetery: MAILLY WOOD CEMETERY, MAILLY-MAILLET, Somme, France

'Another Addlestone soldier to give his life for his country is Pte. Alfred Hill, who was killed instantly by gun shot on June 25th. The deceased, who was attached to the Seaforth Highlanders, enlisted soon after the outbreak of war, and had served in France for something like 13 to 14 months. He was gassed about nine months ago, but shortly after recovery was sent back.

Pte. Hill was the eldest son of Mr. and Mrs. Hill, who until recently resided at Chapel Park, Addlestone, and then removed to Thames Ditton. The unfortunate fellow had been back in France for only two weeks, following a short leave, when he was killed.' (The Surrey Herald, July 21, 1916)

HORN, Harry

Private 17109, 1st Bn. Coldstream Guards
Born in Ottershaw, 1898
Son of Edward and Emily Horn, née Collyer, of Brox Road, Ottershaw (1911 census) (m.1885)
Killed in action, 9 October 1917, Belgium, during the Battle of Poelcappelle, part of the Third Battle of Ypres (Passchendaele), age 19
Memorial: TYNE COT MEMORIAL, Zonnebeke, West-Vlaanderen, Belgium

'We sincerely regret having to record the news of the death in action in France, on 9th October, of Pte. Harry Horn, of the Coldstream Guards, the sixth son of Mr. and Mrs.

Horn, of Brox-road. The sad news reached the parents by letters from an officer and a chum named Adams, who stated that his home was at Addlestone. Both letters were written in a very sympathetic strain, the latter stating that the deceased fell on the 9th October, the day of the new advance.

The late Pte. Horn was only 19 years of age, and it was scarcely six weeks ago that he crossed the Channel, although he had been with the Forces for a couple of years. He was formerly employed at Woburn Place, Addlestone, as under-gardener.

The parents have one other son serving in France with the Yorkshires, and three others are in Mesopotamia and Egypt. The eldest son is in the Royal Navy.' (The Surrey Herald, October 26, 1917)

HUNT, Cecil Alfred
Lance Corporal 320120, 16th (Sussex Yeomanry) Bn. Royal Sussex Regiment
Born in Rhyll, Flintshire, 1896
Son of Arthur Edward and Grace Alice Hunt, née Joel, of Green Lane, Addlestone (m.1895)
Died of wounds, 19 November 1917, in a military hospital in Egypt, age 21
Cemetery: KANTARA WAR MEMORIAL CEMETERY, Egypt

LANGRIDGE, Edward Albert
Private 18350, 3rd Bn. Coldstream Guards
Born in Slaugham, Sussex, 1887
Son of Alfred and Mary Jane Langridge, née Haylor, of Selborne, New Haw Road, Addlestone (1924 Register of Electors) (m.1868); husband of Violet Mary Langridge, née Mason, of Council Cottages, Finchampstead, Wokingham (m.1910)
Killed in action, 1 December 1917, France, during the Battle of Cambrai, while his battalion was attacking German positions near Gouzeaucourt, age 30
Memorial: CAMBRAI MEMORIAL, LOUVERVAL, Nord, France

LAWRENCE, Frederick Charles
Company Quartermaster Sergeant L/9179, 2nd Bn. Queen's (Royal West Surrey Regiment)
Born in Chertsey, 1888
Son of John and Emmeline Mary Lawrence, née Roake, of Stone Hill Road, Ottershaw (1911 census) (m.1888)
Killed in action, 1 July 1916, France, the first day of the Battle of the Somme, during the attack towards Mametz, age 27
Memorial: THIEPVAL MEMORIAL, Somme, France

'OTTERSHAW - A letter has reached the village bearing the information that Co. Sergt. Major Lawrence, of The Queens, was killed in the British advance, but so far no official corroboration has been received by his parents.' (The Surrey Herald, July 21, 1916)

'The casualty lists issued on Sunday contained the name of Co. Q.M.S. Lawrence, of Ottershaw, and the Queen's Royal West Surrey Regt., as having been killed in the British advance. A fortnight ago we published the information that a comrade had written to Mr. and Mrs. Lawrence stating that their son had been killed.' (The Surrey Herald, August 4, 1916)

LONGBOTTOM, William Barnes

Private G/30768, 10th Bn. Queen's Own (Royal West Kent Regiment)
Born in Battersea, 15 September 1899
Foster son of Mrs Sarah Atkins, of Stone Hill Road, Ottershaw (1911 census)
Killed in action, 15 September 1918, Belgium, on his 19th birthday
Cemetery: GROOTEBEEK BRITISH CEMETERY, Poperinge, West-Vlaanderen, Belgium

'Information has been received by Mrs. Atkins, of Stonehill-road, that her adopted son, Pte. W. Longbottom, of the Royal West Kent Regt., was killed by a shell whilst sitting in a small dug-out. This occurred on the 14th September, the day before his 19th birthday. Pte. Longbottom had been in France for five months. Having lived the whole of his life in the village, and been educated at Ottershaw School, he was well known and respected. Prior to joining up he was a gardener at Ottershaw Park, and he had also been with Mr. H. Gosling for some time.' (The Surrey Herald, September 27, 1918)

PURDIE, Robert Henry

Lance Corporal 5421, 2nd Bn. Prince of Wales's Leinster Regiment (Royal Canadians)
Formerly 15967, East Surrey Regiment
Born in Addlestone, 18 March 1896
Son of William and Emily Purdie, née Smart, of Louis Street, Chapeltown Road, Leeds; previously of Chapel Avenue, Addlestone (1901 census)
Killed in action, 12 April 1917, France, during the Battle of Vimy Ridge, part of the Arras offensive, age 21
Cemetery: SUCRERIE CEMETERY, ABLAIN-ST. NAZAIRE, Pas de Calais, France

'Early last week information was received by Mr. and Mrs. Purdie, until recently of Addlestone, that their son, Lc.-Corpl. Robert H. Purdie ("Sonny"), was killed in the advance on April 12th.

Enlisting in the East Surrey Regt., 18 months ago, he shortly afterwards qualified as an instructor of musketry and was promoted Lce.-Corpl. On being sent to the front he was drafted into the Leicester Regt., and to quote from a letter sent by Captain H. R. Buxton, "He obviously died doing his duty magnificently, and he must have been a splendid man to have been an N.C.O. in such a renowned Regt."

Born at Addlestone on the 18th of March, 1896, he had just completed his 21st birthday, and was looking forward to a promising future, having been employed several years as an electrician by the Leytonstone Urban District Council. Amongst his colleagues the news of his death caused the deepest feelings of sympathy and regret.' (The Surrey Herald, May 11, 1917)

'IN MEMORIAM.
PURDIE – In loving memory of Lce.-Corpl. Robert H. Purdie (Sonny) killed in the battle of Arras, April 1917.
At happy moments in your life
It all comes back to me,
When as a boy you laughed and sang
And shouted gleefully.
And when arrived at manhood's age,
Your duty doing well,

Bravely you fought at Arras,
And nobly you fell. – Mother' (The Surrey Herald, April 26, 1918)

RIXON, Theodore Meredith

Lieutenant Colonel, 6th Bn. attd. 8th Bn. King's Royal Rifle Corps
Born in Windsor, abt. 1867
Son of Theodore Robert (d.1883) and Sarah Margaret Rixon, née
Paine, of Surbiton (1901 census); husband of Gladys Mary Rixon, née
Ashburner, of Brighton; previously of Ashdown, Crouch Oak Road,
Addlestone
Killed in action, 19 September 1917, during the Third Battle of Ypres,
age about 50
Awards: MILITARY CROSS; Supplement to the Edinburgh Gazette, August 28, 1916
Cemetery: POELCAPELLE BRITISH CEMETERY, Langemark-Poelkapelle, West-
Vlaanderen, Belgium

*'We understand that Mrs. Rixon, of Ashdown, Crouch Oak-road, has received an
intimation that her husband, Captain T. M. Rixon, has been awarded the Military Cross.
The honour was accorded the gallant officer for having on July 3rd, held a crater with
another officer and five men, during a terrific bombardment.*

*Captain Rixon until just recently had not been in this part of the world for some years
past. He went to Rhodesia in 1893, to take up farming, but when the Matabele rebellions
broke out he fought in both campaigns.*

*When the present war was declared he again joined the British Forces, and fought
against the Huns in the German West African campaign. He the came to England, with
his wife and family, and joined the K.R.R., being sent to France in March. His two
children were both born in Rhodesia.' (The Surrey Herald, September 1, 1916)*

*'Our Addlestone readers will learn with regret of the death, in action in France, of
Lieut.-Col. Theodore Meredith Rixon, M.C., of the King's Royal Rifles, and the eldest son
of Mrs. Theodore Rixon, of Surbiton. The deceased was a brother of Lady Humphery, of
Walton Leigh, and his wife, Mrs Gladys Rixon, who is at present residing at Brighton,
will be recalled by many as residing for some time at Ashdown, Crouch Oak-road.*

*The late Lieut.-Col. Rixon, who was killed on September 19th, was 51 years of age. He
was educated at Merchant Taylors' School, and was one of the original members of the
Old Merchant Taylors' Football Club. For 25 years he lived in Rhodesia, fought in both
Matabele Wars, and assisted in the capture of Lobengula. At the beginning of the war he
enlisted, and went through the German South-West campaign under General Botha.
Returning to England, he was given a commission as captain in the King's Royal Rifles,
afterwards being made major, and eventually given a battalion in that regiment.*

*He crossed over to France in March, 1916, and was awarded the Military Cross on July
3rd of the same year, for having held a crater with another officer and five men, during a
terrific bombardment.' (The Surrey Herald, October 5, 1917)*

'MRS. CAMPBELL, 1896
*Née Gladys Mary Ashburner. Came up with her mother by ox wagon. She became Mrs.
Rixon (Fort Rixon being named after her husband, Colonel Rixon), and later married Mr.
Jock Campbell, also of Fort Rixon. Information, Mr. A. M. Ewing. 'On Roll of Women
Pioneers.' (RootsWeb: SOUTH AFRICA A-L "Rhodesia's Pioneer Women" – Jessie M.
Lloyd)*

72

ROE, Albert John Havilland

Second Lieutenant, 7th Bn. King's Royal Rifle Corps
Born in Bournemouth, 1892
Son of Albert George and Mary Anne Roe, née Dalton, of High Street, Addlestone
(Kelly's Directory 1915)
Killed in action, 9 August 1915, near Hooge, Belgium, age 23
Memorial: YPRES (MENIN GATE) MEMORIAL, Ieper, West-Vlaanderen, Belgium

*'Another Addlestone officer has fallen on the French battlefield, in the person of
Second-Lieut. John Harriland Roe.*

*Lieut. Roe was the only son of Mr. A. Roe, confectioner, of 21 High Street, and was
scarcely twenty-three years of age.*

*The outbreak of the war found him studying at Oxford for the Civil Service, but he
immediately left his books and being a member of the O.T.C. was enabled to obtain a
commission in the King's Royal Rifles.*

*The sad news was received by Mr. Roe during last week, in a letter from the Colonel of
the Regiment, but it does not furnish the date upon which the deceased was killed, or how
he met his death. Lieut. Roe was a prominent Rugby football player.' (The Surrey Herald,
August 20, 1915)*

SIMMONS, Sydney Noel

Lieutenant, Royal Wiltshire Yeomanry
Born in Addlestone, 25 December 1880
Baptised, 16 February 1881, Chertsey
Son of George and Emily Simmons, née Tuppen, of Roydon Lodge, Woburn Hill,
Addlestone (1911 census) (m.1878)
Died of wounds, 27 October 1916, from wounds received during the Battle of the Somme,
age 35
Cemetery: WALTON AND WEYBRIDGE (WEYBRIDGE) CEMETERY, Surrey,
United Kingdom

*'As the result of wounds received on the Somme on August 18th, Lieut. Sydney Noel
Simmons, of the Royal Wilts. Yeomanry, and son of Mr. and Mrs. Simmons, of Roydon
Lodge, Woburn Hill, passed away in London on Friday last.*

*The body was laid to rest in Weybridge cemetery on Monday. The ceremony was
performed by the Rev. Spencer Buller (Rector) and was attended only by the immediate
relatives. The "last post" was sounded by six trumpeters of the 2nd Regt. Royal Wilts.
Yeomanry, who came up from Chippenham. Floral tributes were sent by: Brother officers,
R.W.Y.; Capt. Henderson and officers of D Squadron; Father and mother; Alan and
Winnie; Humphery and Elinor; Enid and Geoffrey; Nurse Piper; W. and Mrs. Blake; Mrs.
and the Misses Kidd; The Countess of Carnarvon; Sir Howard and Lady Elphinston; Mr.
and Mrs. A. Hanney; Babs; Mrs. De Lisle Burns; Mrs and Miss Greenhill; Mrs. Berger,
and Mrs. Butler.' (The Surrey Herald, November 3, 1916)*

*'Throughout this month an interesting exhibition of works by the late Lieut. Noel
Simmons, of Addlestone, is being held in the Mansord Gallery at Heal and Sons, 195
Tottenham Court-road.*

*The exhibition, which consists of pictures and painted furniture, is being held to
"enable those, other than his immediate friends, to appreciate the beginning of what
promised to be a remarkable career. There is an equally developed sense of beauty in*

architecture and in painting, which natural instinct had been enlarged by comprehensive research and study."

The deceased was born on Christmas Day, 1880, at Addlestone, the second son of Mr. and Mrs. Geo. Simmons. At the age of 23 he went to Dominica, in the West Indies, and later continued to paint in France, Morocco and Spain. He joined the Yeomanry in August, 1914, and died of wounds on October 27th, 1916. The number of articles catalogued is 109.' (The Surrey Herald, March 15, 1918)

SLEET, Arthur

Private G/3657, 2nd Bn. Queen's (Royal West Surrey Regiment)
Born in Ottershaw, 1895
Baptised, 30 June 1895, Christ Church, Ottershaw
Son of Frederick and Mary Ann Sleet, née Gillham, of Brox Road,
Ottershaw (1901 census) (m.1890)
Died of wounds, 3 June 1916, France, age 21
Cemetery: CORBIE COMMUNAL CEMETERY EXTENSION,
Somme, France

'Another Ottershaw soldier has given his life for his country in the person of Pte. Arthur Sleet, who succumbed to gunshot wounds in the stomach on June 3rd.

The deceased, who was attached to the Queen's (Royal West Surrey) Regt., enlisted on the 30th Nov., 1914, and after about 12 months training was sent over to France. The son of Mr. and Mrs. Sleet, of Brox Road, and 21 years of age, prior to enlisting he was employed by Messrs. Tarrants, of Byfleet.

The sad news reached Mr. and Mrs. Sleet on Thursday, by means of a letter from the Sister-in-charge of a casualty clearing station.' (The Surrey Herald, June 9, 1916)

SLEET, Frederick

Private G/3659, 1st Bn. Queen's (Royal West Surrey Regiment)
Born in Ottershaw, 1892
Son of Frederick and Mary Ann Sleet, née Gillham, of Brox Road,
Ottershaw (1901 census) (m.1890)
Killed in action, 15 July 1916, in an attack near the village of
Martinpuich, during the Battle of the Somme, age 24
Memorial: THIEPVAL MEMORIAL, Somme, France

'A native of Ottershaw, Pte. F. Sleet, of the 1st Batt. Queen's R.W. Surrey Regt., writes to the Editor from France, expressing the hope that the Ottershaw Service Roll will shortly appear in our columns. After mentioning that he receives the "Surrey Herald" every week, Pte. Sleet continues:-

"I joined the Queen's in November last, and after three months training served with the 2nd Batt., until I had the misfortune to be wounded on 16th May. I was rather disappointed at not rejoining the 2ⁿᵈ Batt., because most of my training chums are there. I have a barn for a billet at the time of writing. The evenings seem rather long, so I wonder if some kind person could send a good mouth organ. We can then have musical evenings. It will not do to get down in the dumps here.

It may interest your readers to know that the children can sing our popular songs quite well. When we are on the march they sing "Tipperary", and call out "Are we downhearted?", and "Shall we Win?" When we answer "No" and "Yes" they give us three hearty cheers." (The Surrey Herald, October 29, 1915)

'We understand that yesterday (Thursday) Mr. and Mrs. Sleet, of Brox Road, received a letter stating that their son, Pte. F. Sleet, of the Queen's Regt., was killed in the British advance on July 1st. But two or three weeks since we reported the death from wounds of another son of Mr. and Mrs. Sleet.' (The Surrey Herald, July 21, 1916)

'It will be recalled by readers that mention was briefly made in our columns recently of the death of Pte. F. Sleet, of the Royal West Surreys, the eldest son of Mr. and Mrs. Sleet, of Brox-road. The parents have now received a letter from a sergeant of the Regiment, and also an official intimation from the War Office. The sergeant explains that the deceased soldier was killed instantly on the 15th July, whilst with an attacking party.

Pte. Sleet enlisted in November, 1914, and in the following March was sent over to France. A couple of months later he received a severe wound in the shoulder, which necessitated his remaining in an English hospital for four months. The deceased was 24 years of age, and prior to enlisting was employed at Fletcher Bros' nurseries. He is the second son Mr. and Mrs. Sleet have lost in the war. It was only as recent as June that the younger son, Arthur, died of wounds. He also belonged to the Royal West Surreys, and was only 21 years of age.' (The Surrey Herald, August 18, 1916)

STEELE, Frederick Arthur Godfrey

Able Seaman J/18803, H.M.S. *Flirt*
Enlisted, 18 July 1912
Born in Weybridge, 17 October 1896
Son of Seth Ormerod and Mary Jane Steele, née Godfrey, of Ham Moor, Addlestone (1901 census) (m.1890); brother of Daisy Marjorie Lea, née Steele, of Ivy Cottage, Lyne, Chertsey (b.1894); brother of Ellen Gertrude White, née Steele, (b.1892)
Died, 26 October 1916, on H.M.S. *Flirt*, age 20
Memorial: PORTSMOUTH NAVAL MEMORIAL, Hampshire, United Kingdom

H.M.S. *Flirt*, a Fawn class destroyer launched in 1897, was sunk at night, off Dover, by German destroyers while attempting to rescue the crew of the sinking drifter *Waveney* that had earlier been attacked by the Germans. Eighty crew members were lost, four survived.

'Among the sailors returned as missing in association with H.M.S. Flirt, which was lost during the Channel raid, was a young fellow who was fairly well known in Ottershaw – Frederick Arthur Godfrey Steele, A.B.

Steele was a brother of Mrs. H. White, who for many years resided in Church-road before leaving for Lower Edmonton, and he spent his holidays in the village. He was on H.M.S. Irresistible when the boat was torpedoed in the Dardanelles on March 18th, 1915.' (The Surrey Herald, November 10, 1916)

TRIGG, Horace

Private T/206666, 2/4th Bn. Queen's (Royal West Surrey Regiment)
Born in Ottershaw, 1882
Son of George and Jane Trigg, née Mant, of Durnford Bridge, Ottershaw (1911 census) (m.1872); 1st cousin of Walter Trigg, also a fatal casualty
Killed in action, 21 December 1917, while fighting against Turkish forces in Palestine, age 35
Cemetery: JERUSALEM WAR CEMETERY, Israel

'Much sympathy will be extended to Mr. and Mrs. George Trigg, of Brox, in the bereavement they have sustained by the death of their elder and only surviving son, Pte.

Horace Trigg, of the Queen's R.W. Surrey Regt. Monday morning brought the sad intimation to the parents, by an official War Office notification, stating that Pte. Trigg was killed whilst fighting with the Egyptian Expeditionary Force on the 22nd Dec.

The deceased, who was 35 years of age prior to enlisting in August, 1915, had been employed by the Staines Linoleum Co. for 17 years. He was drafted to Egypt in February of 1916.

This is the second loss Mr. and Mrs. Trigg have suffered, their younger son, Pte. Sidney Trigg, also of The Queen's, having been killed during the Dardanelles fighting on the 9th August, 1915.' (The Surrey Herald, January 11, 1918)

TRIGG, Sydney

Private T/3706, 2/4th Bn. Queen's (Royal West Surrey Regiment)
Born in Ottershaw, 1889
Son of George and Jane Trigg, née Mant, of Durnford Bridge, Ottershaw (1911 census)
(m.1872); 1st cousin of Walter Trigg, also a fatal casualty
Killed in action, 9 August 1915, near Suvla Bay, on the Gallipoli Peninsula, age 25
Memorial: HELLES MEMORIAL, Turkey

'Information has reached Ottershaw that two young fellows well-known in the village, who enlisted in the 2nd 4th Queen's last autumn, were wounded in the attack launched by that Regiment in the Gallipoli fighting on August 9th.

Pte. L. Gray, writing to his mother from a hospital at Alexandria, states that he has been wounded, though apparently not seriously. He also mentions that Pte. S. Trigg has been severely wounded in the hip.

For some years past Trigg has been a regular member of the cricket team at Ottershaw Park, where he was employed as a gardener, whilst Gray has often appeared in the ranks of the Ottershaw Village C.C.' (The Surrey Herald, September 3, 1915)

TRIGG, Walter

Private 29021, 1/5th Bn. Royal Warwickshire Regiment
Born in Chertsey, 1881
Baptised, 4 December 1881, Christ Church, Ottershaw
Son of Joseph and Emily Trigg, née Joyner, of Union Road, Ottershaw (1911 census)
(m.1872); husband of Georgina Trigg, née White, of Hatchard Road, Upper Holloway, London (m.1906); 1st cousin of Horace and Sydney Trigg, also fatal casualties
Killed in action, 27 August 1917, during the Flanders Offensive, age 36
Cemetery: TYNE COT CEMETERY, Zonnebeke, West-Vlaanderen, Belgium

'Pte. Walter Trigg, of the Warwickshire Regt., and the youngest son of Mr. and Mrs. E. J. Trigg, of Union-road, has also made the supreme sacrifice.

Previously reported by the military authorities as missing after an engagement on the 27th August, the parents have received a further intimation, showing that he was killed in action on that day. Pte. Trigg was 37 years of age and married, his wife residing at Holloway, London. He had only seen about six weeks' fighting at the time he was posted as missing. He leaves a widow and three children.' (The Surrey Herald, November 9, 1917)

UNDERWOOD, Arthur William

Private G/19359, 11th Bn. Queen's Own (Royal West Kent Regiment)
Born in Ottershaw, 1887
Son of Alfred and Elizabeth Underwood, of Stone Hill Road, Ottershaw (1911 census); husband of Lily Constance Watkins, formerly Underwood, née Howe, of Gordon Villas, Broad Lane, Hampton (m.1912)
Killed in action, 31 July 1917, near the village of Hollebeke, during the opening attack of the Third Battle of Ypres (Passchendaele), age 29
Cemetery: VOORMEZEELE ENCLOSURE No. 3, Ieper, West-Vlaanderen, Belgium

UNDERWOOD, Joseph

Private 6019, 1st Bn. Coldstream Guards
Born in Ottershaw, 1886
Baptised, 3 October 1886, Christ Church, Ottershaw
Son of William and Harriett Underwood, née Curtis, of Chobham Road, Ottershaw (1911 census) (m.1867); husband of Emma Underwood, née Sherlock (m.1913)
Killed in action, 22 December 1914, while taking part in an attack near Givenchy, Pas de Calais, France, age 28
Memorial: LE TOURET MEMORIAL, Pas de Calais, France

"Their artillery fire is proper hell upon earth, but their rifle fire is nothing", says Private J. Underwood, of the 1st Coldstream Guards, whose home is at Brox, Ottershaw. Describing his war experiences to a "Surrey Herald" interviewer at his home, he told a vivid tale of battle from the soldier's point of view. A son of Mr. Wm. Underwood, he entered the Army ten years ago, and has for seven years been on the Reserve. He went to France with the 1st Brigade of reinforcements, and was in the first advance movement by the British troops. Wounded in the head on Monday, September 14th, he was sent back to England and then on to Ottershaw for a month's leave.

Asked if he desired to go back, Pte. Underwood replied that he had no wish to – it was too horrible, but he would go willingly when ordered. (The Surrey Herald, October 2, 1914)

'We understand that Pte. J Underwood, of the Coldstream Guards, who was wounded in the early stages of the war, and furnished our readers with some interesting information upon his return home, is now reported as missing by the authorities.' (The Surrey Herald, January 22, 1915)

WEST, Hubert Henry

Sergeant 13350, 8th Bn. Norfolk Regiment
Born in Oxford, 1894
Son of George and Susan West, née Peasley, of The Magnet, Station Road, Addlestone (Kelly's Directory 1915) (m.1881)
Killed in action, 19 July 1916, during the Battle of Delville Wood, one of the Battles of the Somme, age 22
Memorial: THIEPVAL MEMORIAL, Somme, France

'Another Addlestonian has given his life for his country in the person of Sergt. H.H. West, of the Norfolk Regt., the youngest son of Mr. and Mrs. West, of The Magnet public-house.

The deceased enlisted soon after the outbreak of war, and had 12 months service in France to his credit. The notification reached the parents in a letter from the Officer Commanding the Battalion, in which he says – "Your son was killed in action on the 20th July in Delville Wood. At the time of his death, he was gallantly leading his company in a bombing attack, in order to protect the flank of an attacking party; he was hit in the back by a bullet from a German sniper who had stationed himself in a tree. He was instantly killed. He was a brave man, and the whole Battalion mourns his loss."

Sergt. West was 22 years of age, and prior to enlisting was employed as a clerk at Norwich, where he enlisted.' (The Surrey Herald, August 4, 1916)